MISSING THE TIDE

There is a tide in the affairs of men,
Which, taken at the flood, leads on to fortune;
Omitted, all the voyage of their life
Is bound in shallows and in miseries.
On such a full sea are we now afloat,
And we must take the current when it serves,
Or lose our ventures.

William Shakespeare, *Julius Caesar*,
Act 4, scene 3, 218–24

Missing the Tide

Global Governments in Retreat

DONALD J. JOHNSTON

McGill-Queen's University Press
Montreal & Kingston • London • Chicago

© McGill-Queen's University Press 2017

ISBN 978-0-7735-4971-5 (cloth)
ISBN 978-0-7735-4972-2 (ePDF)
ISBN 978-0-7735-4973-9 (ePUB)

Legal deposit second quarter 2017
Bibliothèque nationale du Québec

Printed in Canada on acid-free paper that is 100% ancient forest
free (100% post-consumer recycled), processed chlorine free

McGill-Queen's University Press acknowledges the support of the
Canada Council for the Arts for our publishing program. We also
acknowledge the financial support of the Government of Canada
through the Canada Book Fund for our publishing activities.

Library and Archives Canada Cataloguing in Publication

Johnston, Donald J., author
Missing the tide : global governments in retreat / Donald J. Johnston.

Includes bibliographical references and index.
Issued also in electronic format.
ISBN 978-0-7735-4971-5 (cloth). – ISBN 978-0-7735-4972-2 (ePDF). –
ISBN 978-0-7735-4973-9 (ePUB)

1. World politics – 21st century. I. Title.

D863.J64 2017   909.83'1   C2017-901073-5
                                         C2017-901074-3

This book was typeset in Sabon.

Dedication to Public Servants

The world today finds itself on a number of perilous paths. At such critical times in history, visionary leaders committed to the common good often emerged from the chaos and confusion around them. In the wake of Europe's devastation in the Second World War, for instance, many remarkable individuals, not all of whom were politicians, demonstrated extraordinary and selfless leadership. A good example is Jean Monnet, one of the founding fathers of what became the European Union.

During my career in public life I grew to respect and appreciate the essential role of competent, committed, and honest public servants, who are the infrastructure and operating systems of governments and international organizations. Political leaders may struggle to see beyond the next election cycle, but a core professional public service can provide them with the longer term vision that they need to govern well.

Having dealt with the governments of all OECD countries, I believe without reservation that no government can be better than the quality of its public service.

So I dedicate this book to public servants, who often sacrifice the material rewards of the private sector to serve their fellow citizens. I hope that more of our talented young people will see public service as an honourable and desirable career.

Contents

Acknowledgments

Many have contributed directly and indirectly to the ideas that developed in my mind and through my pen over many years and that coalesced to form the manuscript for *Missing the Tide*.

My wonderful secretary and assistant, Gabriella Goekjian, who died in 2005, encouraged me to write a book as she read my accounts of travels across the globe and meetings with leaders and opinion makers. Over the years I sent her hundreds of pages of notes with detailed accounts and descriptions of people, places, and events.

As the twenty-first century began to unfold it became clear that the world was facing a period of serious and even perilous evolution, far from what we had imagined and hoped for as the twentieth century drew to a close. I began to revisit those dispatches and to reflect on what had happened in the years since.

Many friends and colleagues helped me to refine my reflections on why so much seemed to be unravelling in both the public and private sectors in the early years of the twenty-first century. Several of them offered substantive constructive criticisms that influenced the narrative of this book, often providing insightful evaluations of my conclusions and offering additional ideas. I am particularly grateful to Steve Cutts, Herwig Schlogl, Joanna Shelton, Stan Ridley, Morris Shohet, Graham Watt, Paul Almond, Don Newman, Ray Heard, Stuart (Kip) Cobbett, John McCall MacBain, and Helen Fisher.

Others, such as E. Kaye Fulton, Alex Watt, my wife Heather, and family members were also helpful at different stages in various ways.

I single out Helen Fisher for special mention as she contributed enormously both as an editor and intellectual contributor to many aspects of the final manuscript.

Preface

The purpose of this book is to tell a story, a true but tragic story.

It begins near the end of the twentieth century, a time brimming with optimism about a great future lying ahead for our children and the generations that would follow. They would never witness the brutality and suffering faced by their parents and grandparents nor the abject poverty and misery that had condemned billions of people to lives better imagined than described.

There were a number of major challenges at that time, but it was felt that the world's leaders had the opportunity to not only meet the challenges but to turn them into unprecedented opportunities for rapid and lasting social and economic progress for all humanity. Those challenges and opportunities included geopolitical restructuring in the wake of the fall of the Berlin Wall and the evolution of the European Union; the expansion of the proven Marshall Plan formula to other regions fractured by division and conflict; the exciting prospect of global free trade and investment, which would bring economic growth and rising prosperity everywhere, but especially to the developing world; a long-overdue international commitment to protecting the biosphere and its natural capital; and improvements to the stunning success of healthy capitalism through good governance and appropriate regulatory frameworks across the globe, accompanied by the gradual spread of democracy and transparent, honest government for the benefit of millions of people.

These were the most significant international public policy issues we faced in the latter part of the twentieth century, and they are central to the story outlined in the pages that follow.

Yes, we saw the biosphere deteriorating at a rapid pace, especially through climate change and global warming, but we knew how to fix it and repeatedly said so.

In July 1997 we faced the Asian financial crisis and with the increasing global interdependence of financial markets we feared a global crisis through contagion. But the fear was short lived, and it was thought that the successful containment and resolution of that crisis augured well for the future.

We saw the enormous challenges and wonderful opportunities of globalization moving through many channels: international trade now driven by the World Trade Organization, a creation of the successful Uruguay Round; global investment on a scale not seen since the beginning of the twentieth century; improved and massive transportation networks; and the awesome power of information and communication technologies, together making Marshall McLuhan's global village a reality.

We witnessed the creation of the UN Millennium Development Goals, which were designed to lift billions out of poverty and toward the standards of living of the developed countries.

We also saw the cancer of corruption continuing to limit the growth of emerging market economies and diverting precious foreign aid into the pockets of dishonest public officials in both the developing and developed world. But we were well on our way to securing international agreement through a binding convention to cure that disease.

With the end of the Cold War we foresaw new and promising relations with Russia and China, and the Damocles Sword of massive international armed conflict seemed destined for the dustbin of history.

Hostilities in the Balkans had ceased with the Dayton Accords, and the IRA had laid down its weapons in Northern Ireland. Terrorism was confined to isolated incidents from traditional sources.

Perhaps even more importantly, we saw what we thought was the emergence of democratic government in Russia itself, as well as in other former members of the Soviet Union and countries of Europe that had lived under the Soviet yoke since the end of the Second World War. But the democratic revolution seemed planet wide: countries in South America, Asia, and Africa provided many good examples.

The European Union, and within it the Eurozone, seemed well on the road to creating the largest unified economic market in history, with many countries enjoying the euro as a common currency managed by the European Central Bank.

The world's largest economy, the United States, had brought its public finances under control and was moving into primary surpluses, once again showing the world the benefits of good capitalism at work.

These challenges and opportunities were at the top of the global agenda, and optimism in the mid to late 1990s seemed widely shared across the planet. Sadly it was to be short lived. How, in less than two decades, did our story turn from one of bright hope to one of pessimism and despair?

The environment continues to deteriorate. The outcome of the December 2015 Paris conference, while received with enthusiasm in many quarters, did not produce enforceable solutions, only aspirational hopes that had virtually no possibility of arresting greenhouse gas emissions and then putting them into decline.

Global free trade is in question, as the Doha Development Round launched in 2001 collapsed after 14 years of negotiations in December 2015.

The potential economic and social development of the Arab world and the promise of the Arab Spring have been subsumed by the continuing Palestinian–Israeli conflict and the Sunni–Shia conflict in the breast of Islam, accompanied by international terrorism and the rise of the Islamic State of Iraq and Syria (ISIS).

Vladimir Putin has been fanning the embers of the Cold War and distancing Russia from the West. A new cold war is almost upon us, giving birth to a renewed "arms race" between Russia and the West, but also China.

The financial shenanigans of a greedy few, especially but not exclusively on Wall Street, are threatening the benefits and future of capitalism.

None of the opportunities outlined above has been realized and in some cases they have been completely lost. Much of the wonderful story we told ourselves only 20 years ago is now in a state of shambolic self-destruction.

Why?

In the chapters ahead I focus on the people, policies, and politics that have moved us from where we were to where we are today. Can the rapid decline we have experienced in so many ways, on so many fronts, be arrested and reversed? Sifting through the economic, social, and environmental wreckage, are there lessons to be extracted that will help us collectively to change direction in important ways?

The foregoing paragraphs and the chapters that follow need to be read in the light of some surprising events that have come upon us since this manuscript was finalised. The most surprising, and the one carrying the potential for major global impacts, is the election of Donald Trump as the president of the United States.

It will be some time before we can assess the effect of his policies on the global challenge of climate change considered in chapters 10 and 11 or on the global free trade agenda, which was already under pressure, as detailed in chapter 13, but which he is rapidly moving to undermine by trashing the proposed Trans-Pacific Partnership and threatening to tear up NAFTA. He also appears insensitive to the critical role of the public service by verbally attacking Washington and signing a stream of executive orders to downsize important agencies seemingly on the basis of ideology and ignorance. As I outline in a number of chapters and in the dedication of this book, no government can be better than the quality of its public service. President Trump may not yet understand this.

But more important is his aggressive attack on the fourth estate, the news media. Pamphleteers have played key roles historically in mobilizing public opinion. History illustrates that the pen has indeed been mightier than the sword.

President Trump seems to find support for his views in "alternative facts" and sees the media as the "opposition" with which he declares to be carrying out a running war. Muzzling the media is a characteristic of all authoritarian regimes. America must awaken to the reality that their cherished democracy is threatened by the attacks on this bastion of democracy, namely, the media, which is considered in Chapter 14.

There is no doubt that those who voted for change will get it under the Trump they voted for. But will it be the change they hoped for?

As his term begins I perceive Trump as a "bull in a global china shop." There could be inestimable and largely negative consequences of his presidency.

Beyond the obvious areas of concern signalled by a stream of executive orders, the arrival of a Trump administration heralds a period of global uncertainty on many fronts including relations between the traditional Western allies and Russia and China. Relations with China and especially the Trump administration's aggressive rhetoric challenging China's claims over the South China Sea are particularly ominous.

In essence, the story of global decline outlined in the chapters ahead is more likely to be worse than I envisaged when I thought the manuscript complete, but the areas highlighted remain the same. Therefore, I have made only minor revisions, hoping, as we must, that the tide of opportunities visible at the end of the twentieth century will somehow return, despite the unexpected arrival of Donald Trump as president of the United States.

From right to left on the Opposition benches in Parliament: former Prime Minister John Turner, future Prime Minister Jean Chrétien, and the author (courtesy of Donald J. Johnston)

Author speaking with then-Russian Foreign Minister Yevgeny
Primakov at meeting to discuss Russian accession in Paris
(courtesy of Donald J. Johnston)

Author discussing economics in Dubai with Sheikh Mohammed bin Rashid Al Maktoum, then-Crown Prince of Dubai (courtesy of OECD Photo OCDE/Silvia Thompson)

Author addressing the Munich Security Forum and the potential of applying the Marshall Plan to the Middle East and North Africa region (courtesy of OECD Photo OCDE/Silvia Thompson)

Author speaking with Jacques Delors, former president of the European
Commission, and his wife at Europe Day celebration, Paris
(courtesy of OECD Photo OCDE/Silvia Thompson)

Prime Minister Recep Erdoğan of Turkey addressing OECD ambassadors (courtesy of OECD Photo OCDE/Silvia Thompson)

Author explaining the advantages of the OECD to President Vladimir
Putin of Russia (courtesy of OECD Photo OCDE/Silvia Thompson)

Author on platform with former German Chancellor Helmut Kohl, US President Gerald Ford, US Secretary of Defense Bill Cohen, and others at Arlington National Cemetery for a service commemorating the 50th anniversary of the speech unveiling the Marshall Plan (courtesy of Donald J. Johnston)

Foreign Minister Sergey Lavrov of Russia, author, and OECD Chief
Economist Jean-Philippe Cotis at Moscow meeting (courtesy of OECD
Photo OCDE/Silvia Thompson)

Author meeting Chinese Premier Wen Jiabao at China Development
Forum, Beijing (courtesy of OECD Photo OCDE/Silvia Thompson)

MISSING THE TIDE

I

The Prime Minister Calls

In mid-December 1993 my phone rang and Prime Minister Jean Chrétien was on the line. After a friendly exchange of views and political gossip, he said, "President Clinton has raised with me the prospect of a Canadian becoming head of the OECD. Are you aware of the OECD?"

I was. As a minister in Pierre Elliott Trudeau's cabinet in the Canadian federal government in the early 1980s, I had attended a special Organisation for Economic Co-operation and Development meeting of economic ministers who were wrestling with the challenges of bringing their economies out of the dismal period of stagflation in that era. The period was characterized by high inflation (12 per cent in Canada), soaring interest rates (18 per cent), and virtually no growth.

There was no obvious policy consensus at the time, with the socialist approaches of France and Greece contrasting dramatically with the approaches of the Thatcher and Reagan administrations. It struck me that at the heart of the lack of consensus was a debate between those supporting governments actively intervening as a principal economic player ("faire faire"), such as Mitterrand's nationalization of French banks, and others supporting governments with a market-oriented "laissez faire" approach. Canada's approach fell somewhere in between: I define it as "encourager à faire." This dichotomy remerged in the wake of the 2007–08 recession with the debate over tax cuts and austerity versus public investment.

So I did have first-hand knowledge of the OECD, but only within the macroeconomic context.

The prime minister continued, "The United States wants someone with a political/economic background. You seem to fit the bill, so I am thinking of putting your name forward. Chances of success are 50/50 at most given the European block. There has never been a non-European in the job."

I said I needed a few days to reflect and to discuss it with my wife, Heather. We agreed to go for it.

POLITICAL BACKGROUND

Chrétien and I had been colleagues in the Trudeau cabinet and by and large shared the same economic and social philosophy. John Turner had become prime minister in June 1984, after being elected as leader of the Liberal Party from a field of seven candidates. Chrétien had come second and I had followed in third place.

Brian Mulroney and the Conservatives swept us out of power in the autumn of 1984 and Chrétien resigned his seat in the House of Commons in February 1986. Turner, now leader of the official opposition, and I had been friends for many years. Unfortunately we had a falling-out on two important policy areas.

Mulroney's government brought forward two big ideas: a free trade agreement with the United States, which I supported, and a restructuring of the Canadian Constitution through amendments that became known as the Meech Lake Accord, which I opposed. Turner and most of the Liberal caucus opposed the free trade agreement and he supported the Meech Lake Accord.

This was the most difficult and painful moment of my public life: I found myself holding strong views on two issues that were diametrically opposed to those of the Liberal Party, led by my friend John Turner. Against the opinions of many former colleagues and friends, with a heavy heart I left the Liberal caucus, sat as an independent Liberal in the House of Commons, and voted for the Free Trade Agreement with the United States but against the Meech Lake Accord.

Although my position collided with the position of the Liberal Party at the time, a number of former friends and senior party members asked me to run for the presidency of the party in 1990. It seemed unreal at the time, given my outspoken and widely known opposition to the Turner policies, but in June 1990 I won on the first ballot.

Former Prime Minister Pierre Trudeau turned to me after the vote and remarked, "Well, Don, your position on free trade and Meech Lake seems to have been vindicated by the Liberal Party at the grassroots."

THE CAMPAIGN

In early 1994, shortly after agreeing to stand as a candidate for the position of OECD secretary-general, I was summoned to a meeting at the Department of Foreign Affairs, where I met the deputy minister of the day, Reid Morden. He announced that he was the overall campaign manager of Canada's bid to head the OECD. A senior official, Philip Sommerville, was to be my daily travel companion and adviser in this quest. The Canadian ambassador to the OECD at the time, Anne Marie Doyle, was also a key member of this campaign team.

Off we went. Tokyo, Canberra, Wellington, Washington, London, Bonn, Rome: we visited all 27 member countries of the OECD.

Each government had its own view about the role of the organization. The six non-European members, together contributing more than 50 per cent of the organization's budget, saw it as too Eurocentric.

All countries valued OECD's analytical work, such as the 1994 Jobs Study initiated by my French predecessor, Jean-Claude Paye. The OECD, like governments, is divided into policy silos under specific directorates that have little interaction and do not exploit obvious synergies. Projects with well-defined goals can overcome this problem, which Paye demonstrated with the Jobs Study, an important precedent for cross-cutting work. I had experienced turf protection as a minister responsible for regional development in Canada and was surprised to see the same challenge in an international organization.

A number of countries expressed concern about the possible dilution of OECD values if the organization's membership were expanded, even questioning the value of the organization's work with the rapidly growing Asian Tigers.

My impression was that managing such differing national positions in a consensus organization would be a major challenge. As I travelled from country to country, talking to the policy-makers in numerous ministries, I was puzzled. Like the blind men in the Indian fable who described an elephant as they each touched a different part of the animal, they all had different ideas of what the OECD was and what it did.

Throughout the year-long campaign I regularly received the results of straw polls taken from time to time among the ambassadors at the OECD. All the non-European member countries, including the United States and Japan (together contributing almost 50 per cent of the OECD's budget) supported my candidacy. But Germany, France, and the United Kingdom understandably continued to back their own candidates. The campaign was deadlocked, and restarting the process with new candidates became a real possibility.

Prime Minister Chrétien and Foreign Minister André Ouellet contacted French President Jacques Chirac and Prime Minister Alain Juppé. The deal they brokered was that incumbent Jean-Claude Paye would remain secretary-general for an additional 18 months and I would then assume the post for the normal five-year term, beginning in June 1996.

France then set about convincing their European partners of the merits of this compromise. No one could wish for better support. The French are extraordinary in their diplomacy when it comes to placing candidates, usually French, in positions of international importance.

A German counterpart asked a senior French official why France, given that it headed the International Monetary Fund (IMF; Michel Camdessus), the European Bank for Reconstruction and Development (Jacques De la Rosière), and the European Commission (Jacques Delors), would believe itself entitled to continue to lead the OECD.

The quite admirable reply: "C'est normal."

Finally, late in the year it looked like the compromise was accepted by the membership, but at the eleventh hour Mexico expressed reservations. This came as an unpleasant surprise. Earlier in the year President Salinas had invited me and Canada's ambassador to Mexico, David Winfield, to meet with him at his Los Pinos office in Mexico

City. After friendly and fruitful discussions I had left with the impression that Mexico was supportive. Why the sudden change?

My uncorroborated assumption is that Salinas was seen as a possible candidate to head the World Trade Organization (WTO). His name had been floated by the US secretary of commerce, Mickey Kantor. The Mexicans probably (and correctly) reasoned that if I were to head the OECD another North American had no chance of being chosen to run the WTO.

Finally, late on 30 November 1994, I received a call saying the Mexicans had withdrawn their objection. I was now the secretary-general designate. Prime Minister Chrétien announced the results to the cheers and applause of the political faithful at a Liberal gathering in Toronto, although no more than a handful at best knew what the OECD was or what it did.

THE ILLUSORY OPTIMISM OF THE 1990S

The following decade was remarkable in many ways. The world witnessed a convergence of forces and events that took the globe politically, socially, and economically in directions we had never anticipated.

I arrived in Paris to a world bathed in the comfort of optimism. The recession of the early 1990s was already a distant memory. The potential of innovation and growth through information and communication technologies marched stock markets onward and upward. Millionaires were created daily if not hourly as the Dow and other indexes began their ascent to dizzying heights. One overly enthusiastic observer projected a Dow at 36,000 and others saw the end to business cycles that had bedeviled us in the past. The mid-1990s saw US productivity move to high plateaus judged to be permanent thanks to industries' effective application of more and more information and communication technologies.

The budget of the world's largest economy, the United States, was moving into surplus. At the OECD, the extraordinary Larry Summers led discussions in Working Party 3 (WP3) about whether the United States could manage those future burgeoning surpluses without distorting capital markets.

While some European countries were still dragging their feet on structural reform, especially in labour markets, others were moving forward. The importance of these reforms would later be outlined in the Lisbon Agenda of 2000, which had the ambitious goal of making the European Union (EU) the world's most competitive economy by 2010.

Central European countries were engaging with the West and talking to the OECD about how they could shed the shackles of centralized communist regimes and move rapidly to market economies. Russia was anxious to follow suit and even China was becoming an important interlocutor as it sought to emulate the market economies of the West without the companion of democratic government.

Only Japan continued to languish in pessimism with little economic growth. Suffering a hangover from the collapse of the real estate bubble of the 1980s, major Japanese banks, burdened with non-performing loans, had insufficient capacity to finance struggling companies, especially in the small- and medium-sized business sectors.

For different reasons, economic growth remained sluggish in Europe, but these were, after all, policy challenges requiring major reforms in financial and labour markets, and nothing like the momentous tasks undertaken by the Marshall Plan to successfully address the devastation faced by the previous generation in the wake of the Second World War.

The world was largely at peace. It was Pax Americana, we thought, under the enlightened leadership of US President Bill Clinton's administration. The peace process in Northern Ireland launched in the mid-1990s was a stuttering process but eventually brought peace in 2007 and the British Army ended their mission in Northern Ireland, which had begun in 1969. The Dayton Peace Accords skillfully negotiated by former Swedish Prime Minister Carl Bildt, US Secretary of State Warren Christopher, and Richard Holbrooke in late 1995 had brought the terrible conflict in the Balkans to a close. The IRA ceasefire seemed to be holding, and terrorism was not an issue of global concern. The only visible areas of hostilities were isolated and containable regional conflicts.

Although President Clinton would soon be struggling with personal challenges, the US team was sound: State was led by Warren

Christopher, then Madeleine Albright; Treasury was under the steady hand of Lloyd Bentsen, then Bob Rubin; and the Federal Reserve was skilfully guided by Alan Greenspan.

What I saw and discussed with leaders and senior officials across the OECD membership was the need to address domestic structural challenges among these developed nations, which together represented about 60 per cent of global output. Many of them needed to seize the opportunities offered by globalization while adjusting to the new challenges it presented, especially in labour markets.

During this period the OECD played a key role in a number of major international initiatives that could help all countries benefit from a global economy, and which gave me new perspectives on global issues. Here are some examples:

- supporting the work of the WTO with sound economic analysis of the kind that had enabled agriculture, with its myriad of different domestic support measures, to be included in the recently completed Uruguay Round;
- pursuing a Multilateral Agreement on Investment to complement the global trade agenda;
- attacking corruption in international transactions where bribery was undermining honest trade and diverting development aid from its intended beneficiaries to the secret bank accounts of crooked politicians and public officials (this would result in the OECD Anti-Bribery Convention);
- supporting sustainable development through work on the environment and analysis of the interface between the environment, economic growth, and social cohesion;
- addressing harmful tax practices that were syphoning vast sums into tax havens, sometimes legally but often illegally, and hidden behind a wall of bank secrecy in many countries;
- reaching out to non-member economies, helping some prepare for membership in the WTO or the OECD, to take advantage of the opportunities in rapidly liberalizing global markets; and

- opening the benefits of these markets to developing countries through trade and ensuring that development aid was
  not squandered on donors' supply-driven interests.

All of these objectives could be seen as an application of the principles of the Marshall Plan in a global context. The Plan is addressed
in more detail in the next chapter.

OPTIMISM TO PESSIMISM AND US DECLINE

Sadly, what looked in the late 1990s to be a prolonged period of
peace, growth, prosperity, and expanding world trade with the completion of the Uruguay Round and the creation of the WTO in 1994
did not evolve as we had imagined. The collapse of the high-tech
stock market bubble, a wave of massive corporate scandals, and the
cancer of terrorism shifted the very comfortable paradigm. The resid-
ual effects of 9/11 and the reaction to it remain with the world to this
day and will probably do so well into the future.

We saw the United States as a lone global superpower, magnan-
imous and fair, the first true "united nation" with people from all
corners of the planet drawn to its robust democracy and unlimited
opportunity. That was all to change quickly.

The invasion of Iraq made it impossible to reconcile the actions of
the US administration of George W. Bush with the prevailing view of
the American Gentle Giant. With a number of my OECD colleagues, I
watched Colin Powell's speech to the United Nations Security Council about the threat of Iraq and its alleged weapons of mass destruction. We were all skeptical and unconvinced after his presentation.
There was good reason for our misgivings, as we were soon to learn.
Couple the US stance on Iraq with mounting concern about frugality
with the truth, unauthorized wiretapping, political corruption, and
the censoring of scientific findings, and international public opinion
of America suddenly plunged.

Fortunately many, if not most, Americans began to take a hard
look at the slick salesmanship that had brought them to this level of
international disdain. Adding to their concerns, domestic fiscal policy

favoured the affluent with tax cuts while driving the country deeper and deeper into debt, largely through military expenditures on the worst American foreign policy adventure in history. Then, in 2005, came Hurricane Katrina. The level of physical damage and personal misery in Louisiana exposed the weak underbelly of poverty in the United States and the fragility of the longer term social contract.

Faith in America as a long-surviving empire was seriously shaken. Suddenly its self-proclaimed and widely welcomed role as the benign leader spreading democracy and good governance around the globe was in question.

At the same time we saw America flexing its muscles in international trade negotiations. Claiming to be a proponent and defender of multilateral trade, the United States continued to pursue and exploit bilateral trade and investment agreements. After all, it was the proverbial 800-pound gorilla. Why not pick off 100 smaller gorillas one by one rather than entering a ring with all of them at the same time?

In fairness, any country with the negotiating power of the United States would probably have done the same. But what we witnessed in this unipolar world dominated by one economic behemoth clearly showed that the multipolar universe must play a significant role if multilateralism is to have a future.

That is bound to happen, I thought, watching the accelerating decline in America's influence, if China rises and Europe gets its act together as a coherent global federal force. Even Japan, the weak performer during the "lost decade" of the 1990s, had started to show some sustained recovery.

While American excellence remains in almost every area of human endeavour, it rests upon fragile foundations that today are showing fault lines that could tear apart the social fabric. Income and wealth disparities are increasing at an accelerating rate. A rapacious financial community is abusing the opportunities of capitalism. Many of those who gained huge wealth and influence through the benefits of capitalism, and who should be its defenders, are exploiting short-term opportunities with unethical conduct rather than promoting the long-term prosperity and societal benefits that capitalism has provided.

The education system is failing to deliver the necessary knowledge and skills to millions of young people, and the political system lurches from crisis to crisis, threatening to bring the government to a standstill through political gridlock. Also worrisome is the tendency to "money politics" where high electoral office is increasingly reserved for the wealthy, well-connected political elite. Combine that trend with the validation of the unlimited capacity of super PACs (political action committees) to intervene financially in the democratic process, and where will the once-great American democracy find itself? How can the best and the brightest be attracted to seek elected office within the political system we see evolving?

The United States is by no means the only society facing threats to its economic and social progress, but its continuing preponderant position in today's world merits special scrutiny as we look to the future. As Keynes reminded us, we should examine the present in light of the past for the purposes of the future.

Historically the United States has had an extraordinary capacity to recover, heal its wounds, and move forward. My maternal grandmother was born before the American Civil War, which claimed 600,000 lives (on a population base of only 31.4 million people, of whom 12.7 per cent were slaves) and caused untold physical damage. Reflecting upon the explosion of development that quickly followed, how can we not be optimistic about where America will go in this twenty-first century?

As the sage of Omaha, Warren Buffett, says, "Never bet against America."

Yes, but that optimism must today be tempered by profound concerns about the US political system, which is contributing to inequality on a scale never seen before. I consider this issue below. It also seems to be a preoccupation of Buffett himself, to his credit.

LOSING THE BALANCE

One of the lessons I have drawn from observing the rise and fall of political parties and their governments is the necessity for good governance to balance economic growth and wealth creation with

Figure 1.1

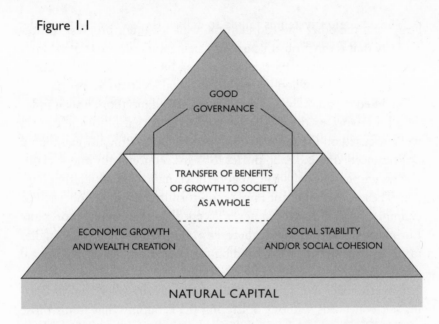

social cohesion, all founded on the planet's natural capital, meaning a healthy and protected environment (figure 1.1). The components of natural capital are the soil, air, water, and biodiversity, the latter comprising all living things. Currently each of these components is threatened at the global level.

While a single nation can balance the economic and social dimensions of its societal progress through good governance, and while it can green its own economic development, working alone that nation cannot prevent the consequences of global warming and other challenges threatening the planet's sustainable development.

When growth and social cohesion are balanced, societies progress. If they are not, societies slow, stop, or implode through revolution, notably in non-democratic countries or those with immature democracies, such as Thailand. History is replete with examples, none better than the French Revolution, the collapse of the Soviet Union, the fall of the Berlin Wall, and more recently the Arab Spring.

In discussions with the Canadian prime minister at the time, Pierre Trudeau, I described the balance as a challenge for governments not unlike that of a tightrope walker. If one end of the balancing pole is too heavy and the other end too light the walker cannot progress. Unfortunately that is the problem currently facing not only the United States (where the problem is particularly acute), but also many other countries globally: two billion people still exist on less than $2 per day.

He liked the analogy and periodically asked me about how it influenced my work at the OECD. My answer was that all of the OECD's work focused on maintaining that balance by continually examining policies needed to move countries forward economically and socially, always emphasizing the role of good governance in making that happen. These efforts did not imply a uniformity of public policies. For example, Americans would never accept the taxation levels of many European countries where there is a cultural tolerance for higher taxation to support public funding for education, health, and social safety nets.

Governments will fail, and fall, if they focus solely on addressing societal needs without bolstering the economy that funds those efforts. The same is true if there is growth but no perceived benefit to society as a whole. This is the risk currently run by a number of countries where income and wealth seem locked into a steady increase, but only for the infamous 1 per cent.

To make this more meaningful, look at history's most successful economy and robust democracy. Despite the economic turndown of recent years, wealthy Americans have become even richer. The GDP of the United States in 1980 was between $2 trillion and $3 trillion. By 2014 it was estimated to be $17.7 trillion or 22 per cent of global GDP. By contrast, real wages over that period only rose from $20,959 to $28,829 (in 2013 dollars). There was a slight but welcome improvement in wages in 2015, but it only took the average American household back to close to its 2008 income. Ordinary American workers remain angry and frustrated.

Is that trend sustainable? I think not. The Republican and Democratic 2016 presidential primaries, where two outsiders, Donald Trump and Senator Bernie Sanders, each found huge support on opposite sides of the political divide, point to deep anger and frustration in the US population. The truth of the saying often invoked by John Kennedy, "a rising tide lifts all boats," is questionable in the United States and in many other countries. "A rising tide lifts all yachts" seems to have more currency today.

Nobel Prize winner Joe Stiglitz has identified the society-wide negative impacts of this growing problem in his book *The Price of Inequality: How Today's Divided Society Endangers Our Future* (W.W. Norton, 2012). He writes that "politics have shaped the market, and shaped it in ways that advantage the top at the expense of the rest." He also says, "By 2007 the average after-tax income of the top 1 percent had reached $1.3 million, but that of the bottom 20 percent amounted to only $17,800. The top 1 percent get in one week 40 percent more than the bottom 20 percent receive in a year."

It is obvious that the political system in the United States must be overhauled before the democracy is destroyed by financing mechanisms such as the use of super PACs to raise unlimited funds from businesses, unions, or individuals to support or oppose particular candidates. In a wealthy country like the United States this has not only kept good candidates from running, it has also created a society where governments have been hijacked by the affluent and we increasingly see government of the rich, by the rich, and for the rich.

The rich beneficiaries of the current system seem insensitive to the long-term consequences of the loss of the balance illustrated in figure 1.1. Will there be a dangerous lurch to the left through the electoral process, or will the electoral process be so impotent as to invite more radical reactions, even violence, beyond the peaceful demonstrations of Occupy Wall Street?

Looking at the application of the Gini coefficient to the United States, Erik Sherman had this to say in *Fortune* (30 September 2015): "And yet, with the overall growth of wealth, inequality remains a persistent issue, especially in the United States. For the first time in this report series, Allianz calculated each country's wealth Gini coefficient – a measure of inequality in which 0 is perfect equality and 100 would mean perfect inequality, or one person owning all the wealth. It found that the US had the most wealth inequality, with a score of 80.56, showing the most concentration of overall wealth in the hands of the proportionately fewest people."

It is incredible that the wealthiest country in history has the highest level of wealth inequality. What is more incredible is that most of the rich do not seem to give a damn. The price of inequality about which Stiglitz writes is very high and portends very unpleasant and disruptive economic and social consequences for the next generation.

The recent presidential election in the United States serves as an important lesson. Against all expectations and polls and contrary to the opinions of important pundits, an outsider, Donald Trump became president of the United States. Why? Because Americans are fed up with the situation described above, where democracy has been hijacked through money politics to make America a government of the rich, by the rich, and for the rich. It was not sustainable. Now, will the Trump administration correct this crumbling of a once-great democracy or will it, like others, be seduced by the extraordinary wealth of some Americans instead of being motivated to address the poverty and disillusionment of millions who supported Trump? Trump's supporters have high expectations of change for the better. Will those be met? We will not know for some years, which may be characterized by great uncertainty about this wonderful democracy that must once again heal itself.

I think it will happen. Remember Buffett's words: "Never bet against America."

A FUTURE THREATENED

However, the promising future we foresaw at the end of the twentieth century is now threatened in part by economic slowdown or contraction with a decrease in employment opportunities in many sectors, but principally by the alienation of very large segments of society who are being left behind. They know it and they are determined to do something about it. This is evidenced by the Brexit vote in the United Kingdom followed by the Trump victory in the United States, which had been considered to be unthinkable.

The failure to deal with other issues, including climate change, regulation of the financial sector, declining international trade and investment, regional conflicts, and increasing terrorism, is casting a long shadow over the future we envisioned when I arrived in Paris in 1996.

What lessons can we draw from so many failures? Will those lessons help put the world back on the track of increasing global prosperity, eradicating poverty, and ensuring global peace? These questions are explored in the following pages.

2

The Genius of Jean Monnet and the Marshall Plan

The Marshall Plan was one of the greatest political and economic successes of the twentieth century. It serves as a precedent for the establishment of stability and security in other parts of the world.

CELEBRATING FIFTY YEARS OF
CO-OPERATION AND ECONOMIC SUCCESS

On 7 June 1997 there was a ceremony at Arlington National Cemetery to mark the fiftieth anniversary of the Harvard speech during which George Marshall unveiled his plan. As head of the OECD, the living legacy of the Marshall Plan, I was privileged to attend this historic event. Joining former President Gerald Ford, Defense Secretary Bill Cohen, and others, I listened as German Chancellor Helmut Kohl talked about the importance of the generous Marshall Plan to rebuilding a strong and stable Europe. His personal recollections of being a child looking to the plan for basic nutrition were touching. Assessing his physical stature that day made me think that the plan had exceeded expectations.

In Marshall's memory we planted a tree close to his grave before taking our places on the rostrum. Before this, we gathered in a small tent where coffee and refreshments were served. When President Ford realized I had been a member of Pierre Trudeau's cabinet he took me aside and told me that he and Trudeau were not only good friends but that he had really brought Canada into the G7. He said that when the leaders of the G6 met at Rambouillet in France in 1975 under the chairmanship of President Giscard d'Estaing he felt that the group, consisting of France, Germany, Italy, the United Kingdom, Japan, and the United States, was too Eurocentric and the addition of Canada would provide some balance. With the unanimous consent of the others he immediately contacted Trudeau, who agreed to Canada joining the group. The group became the G7 the following year.

The ceremony in 1997 in Washington also served to underline the strong ties between the United States and Europe that the Marshall Plan had nurtured, ties that were to be sorely tested a few years later by the decision of the George W. Bush administration to invade Iraq. Sitting in the beautiful Benjamin Franklin Room of the State Department, listening to historian Stephen Ambrose's luncheon address on the Marshall Plan, we reflected upon the policies that had united post-war Europe.

The genius of the Marshall Plan was its legacy, part of which was the physical infrastructure that resulted from the investment of billions of dollars administered under the plan and the contribution these investments made to rebuilding Europe in the wake of the devastation of the Second World War. The other part, of even greater value, was the recognition that lasting peace, prosperity, and security on the European continent would only be acquired through economic development, co-operation, collaboration, and economic interdependence. That is the legacy that must be carried forward to future generations not only in Europe but all over the world.

The very existence of the EU will be seen by future historians as a remarkable example of human ingenuity. The violent history from which it was born in a compressed time frame is utterly breathtaking. British historian H.A.L. Fisher provides some perspective and context in the introduction to his work *A History of Europe* (Houghton Mifflin Co., 1936) about the differences that divided Europe's peoples in 1936.

These differences are unresolved. One by one the great attempts to impose a common system upon the energetic self-willed peoples of Europe have broken down. The Roman Empire was foiled by the Germans. The Christian Church, by far the most powerful of the influences which in historical times has worked for union, was ruptured first by the quarrel between the Greeks and the Latins, and then by the revolt of the Protestant north. Nor has any system of secular ideas been more successful in obtaining universal acceptance. Europe refused to be unified by the egalitarian plan of the French Revolution. Equally it now declines to accept the iron programme of Russian Communism. Yet ever since the first century of our era the dream of unity has hovered over the scene and haunted the imagination of statesmen and peoples. Nor is there any question more pertinent to the future welfare of the world than how the nations of Europe, whose differences are so many and so inveterate, may best be combined into some stable organization for the pursuit of their common interests and the avoidance of strife.

A few years later the world was torn apart by the horrors of the Second World War. Fisher's assertion that no question would be "more pertinent to the future welfare of the world than how the nations of Europe ... may best be combined into some stable organization for the pursuit of their common interests and the avoidance of strife" remains important and prescient.

Even in their most ambitious flights of imagination, the world leaders of the late 1930s could not have predicted what would happen in the aftermath of the war, as the thunder of impending conflict rumbled across Europe and around the world. What forces, what events, what philosophy, and what people enabled this dream of unity to become a reality?

LESSONS FROM VISIONARY LEADERS

Above all, unity required the catalytic role of visionaries in a position to make things happen. The world was fortunate that there were people such as George Marshall and Jean Monnet. History tells us that people of such quality and vision often emerge when destiny beckons. So it was in the wake of the Second World War.

They were remarkable individuals, but they were not alone. There

were political leaders, especially President Truman and C[...]
lor Adenauer, but also key players like Georges-Augustin Bida[...] .....
Robert Schuman who had the courage and foresight to stake out an
enduring future for Europe that continues to evolve despite the current challenges of the EU and the eurozone. In the great scheme of
things history will record these as bumps on the road to a dynamic
and prosperous Europe.

Jean Monnet enjoys a special place in history. He saw that economic interdependence was the key to peace, security, and prosperity.
Monnet's coal and steel plan, which created the European Coal and
Steel Community (ECSC) for Western Europe, may have seemed modest at the time, but in the words of then-US Secretary of State Dean
Acheson, "it was in reality imaginative and far reaching, because it
picked out of the basic materials of Europe's industrial economy, coal
and steel, to put under the supranational control of an organization
of the participating European States" (*Present at the Creation*, W. W.
Norton & Co., 1987).

The ECSC laid the foundations of a united Europe, which was
Monnet's ambition. A statement by the French government at the
time concluded that "the pooling of coal and steel production should
immediately provide for the setting up of common foundations for
economic development as a first step in the Federation of Europe,
and will change the destinies of those regions which have long been
devoted to the manufacture of munitions of war, of which they have
been the most constant victims." The words "as a first step in the Federation of Europe" in the communiqué are significant today because
this particular "F" word seems to be widely controversial; this subject is addressed in the next chapter.

As the poet David Everett wrote, "Large streams from little foun-
tains flow, tall oaks from little acorns grow." This thought was not
wasted on Monnet, who saw the ECSC as the acorn from which the
EU would grow through economic interdependence. The ECSC was
the first of the supranational building blocks that became the European Economic Community and then the Union.

The Marshall Plan benefited from a broader government understanding of the constituent elements of economic growth than had

existed in the past. Economic historians such as Robert Heilbroner and Angus Maddison have shown that the open market system and wealth creation were poorly understood before the eighteenth century. Writing in the late 1990s, Maddison says, "From 1500 to 1820 the average growth of world per capita income was only a thirtieth of that achieved since 1820" (*The World Economy: A Millennial Perspective*, OECD, 2001).

The market system transformed our societies. It confronted, even destroyed, traditional thinking; it drove innovation, the "creative destruction" of Joseph Schumpeter. It resulted in accelerating change and economic growth on a scale never before imagined. This was well understood by the architects of post-war Europe. Even pre-war isolationist US Senator Arthur Vandenberg supported the Marshall Plan because he recognized that a strong, united Europe was an important asset for US trade and economic development.

The magic of the market system has accelerated the material progress of the human race at a pace difficult to comprehend. Creative destruction through innovation has improved most aspects of our lives; better health, safer cars, and faster communication tools are but a few examples. In 1965, Intel co-founder Gordon Moore predicted that the number of transistors in a dense integrated circuit would double approximately every two years, a prediction that became known as Moore's law and that proved accurate for many decades. In its 19 April 2015 edition, the *Economist* suggested that Moore's law may come to an end, not because transistors cannot technically be shrunk further, but because of their increased cost. This is the market system at work.

EXPANDING THE CONCEPT TO THE WORLD

What does all this mean in terms of the Marshall legacy? Open market economics took hold in the nineteenth century and into the twentieth century. Political leaders and economists during the post-war period understood that only through broadening market integration and economic interdependence would Europe become the economic power it is today.

In recent years, we have indeed witnessed new examples of regional economic co-operation and integration that have used the approach of the Marshall Plan, such as the Stability Pact for the Balkans. This ambitious program was launched in July 1999 when world leaders and the heads of international organizations gathered in the Sarajevo arena that had been constructed for the 1984 Olympics.

Given the location in Sarajevo and the list of attendees, which included some forty leaders and senior officials, the security measures exceeded anything I had encountered to that point. For that reason twenty or more of us were flown out to Sarajevo from Rome on the morning of the meeting in a well-armed British military Hercules aircraft. Among my fellow passengers were Canadian Prime Minister Jean Chrétien and Chancellor Viktor Klima of Austria, whom I had known from his previous role as minister of finance. Given that we were travelling on a military aircraft, the facilities were quite primitive. A crew member showed us the location of the sole toilet, which sat conspicuously a few metres in front of all the seated passengers. Privacy was ensured by a pull-around plastic curtain secured on a makeshift circular curtain rod. Fortunately the flight was not too long, but it was not surprising that none of these distinguished personages chose to avail themselves of the toilet. There was probably a rush to the washrooms at Sarajevo upon our arrival.

THE BALKANS, THE MIDDLE EAST AND NORTH AFRICA PROJECT, AND BEYOND

As Finland held the presidency of the EU at the time of the Sarajevo meeting, President Martti Ahtisaari chaired the meeting. A knowledgeable and energetic president and diplomat, Ahtisaari later earned the Nobel Peace Prize (in 2008) for his tireless efforts to bring peace and security across the globe.

Because I was head of the OECD, the organization that represented the living legacy of the Marshall Plan, Ahtisaari invited me to address this impressive gathering. Using the success of the Marshall Plan as a convincing precedent, I emphasized that an integrated open market environment would ensure stability and future economic growth for the Balkans.

As we exited the arena President Clinton congratulated me on the substance of the comments and the fact that I had delivered many of them in French. I had done so because it was one of our two OECD official languages and President Jacques Chirac was present.

The philosophy and methodology of the Marshall Plan was also brought to the Middle East and North Africa (MENA) project. In co-operation with the United Nations Development Programme (UNDP) and the European Commission, the OECD engaged in the MENA project, a Marshall-type approach to the economic development challenges of the Middle East and North Africa. A framework for dialogue and co-operation was presented in Rabat. This initiative showed great promise, even in the shadow of the Iraq war, and concrete steps were taken to move it forward.

Then, in the spring of 1995, I had the privilege of joining and addressing Jordan's King Abdullah and prime ministers and ministers from 18 Arab states in a meeting hosted by the king at the Dead Sea Conference Centre. They had gathered to launch a program to promote good governance for development among Arab states, with the support of the United Nations Development Programme, the Arab League, the World Bank, the OECD, and others.

This regional effort, led by Arab countries, was designed to stimulate and support the implementation of policies to improve the effectiveness and responsiveness of their governments. The resulting Good Governance for Development Program was part of a MENA-OECD initiative that also included a program aimed at improving the investment climate with appropriate policy frameworks.

Clearly there was broad political interest in understanding why the Marshall Plan was an enduring success by reason of policies, not money. I explained the MENA initiative to the Broader MENA Investment Conference in Munich in 2005 and met in Riyadh with Saudi King Abdullah, then the crown prince, where we had an extensive discussion about investment incentives. He had no interest in the parallel governance project, which I thought was a bad sign. Fortunately, there were leaders in the MENA region, many of them young, well-educated, and dynamic, who seemed willing to take forceful action to improve both governance and the investment climate in their respective countries.

Where this ambitious project will lead in the light of the unfulfilled promise of the Arab Spring, the turmoil in much of the Middle East, and the rise of ISIS remains a moot point. It appears to have been recast as a MENA-OECD Governance Programme, that is, a partnership between MENA and OECD countries to share knowledge and expertise. The threats posed by ISIS to both regional and global stability are arresting the near-term success of a MENA region that has the potential to be an integrated, powerful, stable, and economically and socially developed powerhouse within the international community of advanced nations.

Depending upon the outcome, there could be extraordinary potential for economic development within the region, carrying with it prospects for economic growth, the building of comparative advantages, and the elimination of barriers to trade and investment, which would build a strong regional economy tied into the global economy. Peace and security would accompany these changes.

Ultimately, with good progress in the peace process, Israel could become an active member of the MENA initiative. Is that likely? During a discussion on the MENA initiative at Davos, the now-disgraced but talented Ehud Olmert of Israel (currently serving a prison term for corruption) pointed out to Arab leaders including the secretary general of the Arab League, Amr Moussa, how much comparative advantage Israel could offer to the MENA region, given his country's leading-edge global technology in many areas, including water irrigation and desalination and medicine. All present agreed, but Moussa said bluntly, "Not until a Palestinian–Israeli peace initiative gains traction."

Europe rose from the ashes of war through the positive interplay of economic development and security and the recognition that the prosperity of each country depends upon the financial and societal prosperity of its trading partners. Global success depends on the same factors. We are on our way, but, as the challenges of the MENA region all too clearly illustrate, there remains much to be done to establish a truly global integrated market system. Moreover, as I point out in chapter 13, the ambitious program of multilateral trade has begun to unravel in a number of ways and indeed may find major opposition in the post-Obama administration in the United States if the protectionist policies advanced by President Trump are in fact implemented.

3

Europe Listing, but Afloat

[No] question [would be] more pertinent to the future welfare of
the world than how the nations of Europe ... may best be combined
into some stable organization for the pursuit of their common interests and the avoidance of strife.

H.A.L. Fisher, *A History of Europe*, 1936

BREXIT: THE APPARENT PLEASURE OF EUROSKEPTICS

Although I have lauded the Marshall Plan's amazing contribution
to the Europe of today, it is clear that Fisher's vision of a strong,
unified Europe remains very much a work in progress. Yet I remain
convinced that Fisher was right, and the great rebuilding of Europe
after the Second World War must and will endure notwithstanding
the barrage of euroskeptic critics, now emboldened by the United
Kingdom's Brexit vote of June 2016. Admittedly this conviction is
based on Europe having strong, visionary leadership, which has not
yet materialized.

Although Greece represents less than 3 per cent of the Euro zone
economy, euroskeptics used its financial crisis as ammunition to predict its withdrawal from the eurozone and the possible unravelling of
the entire EU. The Greeks rejected that option: there was no Grexit.
The Austrians also rejected right-wing populist nationalism in the
2016 presidential election.

The support for Brexit in the UK referendum was an unexpected
shock for some, but it pleased others who wish to see the EU unravel
and claim that the UK attitude reflects views held in other major
European countries. I keep hearing and reading that the United
Kingdom has rejected the EU, as if it were an overwhelming victory.

Brexiters seem to ignore the fact that of 33,551,984 votes cast (representing just over 72 per cent of registered voters) only 17,410,742 voted to exit the EU. The difference between those voting to leave and those voting to stay was a mere 1,269,500 votes. It might well have been a very different result had there not been such confidence before the referendum that Brexit would be defeated.

REVERSION TO SOVEREIGN NATIONS

In an interesting commentary in *Foreign Affairs* (summer 2016), Professor Jakub Grygiel implies that the upside to the EU crisis will be a return to independent sovereign nation-states across Europe. That would be an upside for American isolationists. It would remove from US competition the largest unified single market in history and reinstate the possibility of future wars on the continent that this great European experiment was designed to prevent – as it has.

Some of Grygiel's comments appear designed to create a false impression of the views of Europeans. Here is a cheerful observation to support his thesis: "a Europe of newly assertive nation-states would be preferable to the disjointed, ineffectual, and unpopular EU of today. There's good reason to believe that European countries would do a better job of checking Russia, managing the migrant crisis, and combating terrorism on their own than they have done under the auspices of the EU."

Really? What is that "good reason" that escaped the attention of the statesmen and nation builders like Jean Monnet in post-war Europe? Grygiel also says that the EU is ineffectual, which is true in some cases as it is with all supranational bodies, including much of the United Nations (UN) activities. However, it is interesting to note successes that the EU has achieved, one good example being the collective research of 28 European countries collaborating to produce one-third of the world research's output – 34 per cent more than the United States and more than China (*New Scientist* [4 June 2016]: 18). These are the kind of synergies that could be sacrificed should the EU dissolve.

THE FALSE PROMISES OF BREXIT

The United Kingdom was the only country where polls supported an exit policy, and even there the slim margin of the result suggests the outcome would have been different had the voters turned out and had leaders of the exit movement not wildly misrepresented the financial implications for the United Kingdom. Note the following comment from the outstanding economic columnist Martin Wolf in the *Financial Times* (24 June 2016):

> David Cameron took a huge gamble and lost. The fear mongering and outright lies of Boris Johnson, Michael Gove, Nigel Farage, *The Sun* and the *Daily Mail* have won. The UK, Europe, the West and the world are damaged. The UK is diminished and seems likely soon to be divided. Europe has lost its second-biggest and most outward-looking power. The hinge between the EU and the English-speaking powers has been snapped. This is probably the most disastrous single event in British history since the Second World War.
>
> Yet the UK might not be the last country to suffer such an earthquake. Similar movements of the enraged exist elsewhere – most notably in the US and France. Britain has led the way over the cliff. Others might follow.

THE EU AS A GLOBAL SUPERPOWER

Will others follow the United Kingdom over the cliff? Alina Polyakova and Neil Fligstein, in the *International New York Times* of 6 July 2016, rely on recent polls that suggest that will not happen. They say, "Britain is not, and never has been, a typical member of the European Union, and in no country but Britain do populists and other Euroskeptic forces have the 51 percent of votes needed to pull their countries from the union."

As for Professor Grygiel's comments on the strength of patriotism in European nations versus attachment to Europe, polling results cited by the authors do not support his view: "Britons have long been more nationalistic than other Europeans. In 2015, 64 percent of British citizens said they would identify as British over European, compared with only 36 percent of Frenchmen, 26 percent of the Dutch and 25 percent of Germans, according to the Eurobarometer, the [well-respected] European Commission's public opinion survey."

BREXIT MAY NOT HAPPEN

At the 2016 World Knowledge Forum in Seoul, South Korea, in October, I was invited to join a panel as the only non-European to discuss the world after Brexit. The other members of the panel were three former European prime ministers, George Papandreou (Greece), Carl Bildt (Sweden), and Esko Aho (Finland). The moderator was Nik Gowing of the BBC.

Gowing began the session with a question to me about where I saw the status of Brexit today. It seemed to surprise most present, including the largely Korean audience, when I replied, "I do not think that Brexit will happen. Although Prime Minister May has declared that she will invoke Article 50, which is required to exit the EU by next March (2017), that is only the beginning of a process. Negotiations on the terms then ensue and they are supposed to close within 2 years. Anytime within that period the UK can change its mind and remain in the EU."

However, this question seems to be at the centre of a legal debate, with many arguing that after Article 50 is triggered it is not reversible. I explained that the United Kingdom was likely to change its mind for many reasons.

First, the referendum vote was a razor-thin victory: 51.9 per cent of eligible voters voted for Brexit and 48.1 per cent voted to remain.

Second, only 72 per cent of eligible voters actually voted. This is a high turnout by normal election standards but surely not in a national game-changing referendum, especially where it appears that most people assumed, like Prime Minister Cameron, that Brexit would be defeated.

Third, it was a vote of passion, not reason, to some extent based on falsehoods, as Martin Wolf pointed out in the comment above. Over the ensuing months and years but before Brexit takes effect, people in the United Kingdom will begin to painfully learn facts about which they should have been aware before the referendum. There are many examples, but one is startling. Brexiters were motivated, according to Baroness Ashton, by three factors: defending borders (i.e., not accepting freedom of movement within the EU and immigrant inflow), not sending funds to Brussels, and independence. The immigration issue was very prominent. However, the reality is that two-thirds of immigration to the United Kingdom within the last decade came from non-EU countries. There the United Kingdom can "defend its borders," so is the EU to blame? And have immigrants not made a huge contribution to the UK economy and society without adding to the cost of unemployment benefits? At the time of the referendum in June 2016, the unemployment rate in the United Kingdom was a mere 4.9 per cent. What countries would not envy that number?

Fourth, many other negative facts will be exposed in the months and years ahead with electoral politics looming in the background. Two months is a long time in politics, never mind two years. What government would have the courage to sign off on Brexit if the polls show a large majority of electors opposed, which is likely to be the case when the consequences are better understood? However, if it is not reversible then Brexit may happen against the will of the majority of people in the United Kingdom.

I was surprised when two of my colleagues on the panel, Esko Aho and George Papandreou, agreed with me. Carl Bildt believed Brexit will happen.

Unfortunately this will be a very difficult period for businesses in the United Kingdom and their employees as more potential investors put plans on hold because of uncertainty and others elect to leave for the continent to protect the markets they have developed from a UK base. As an example, a poll in the *Financial Times* in December 2016 reported that "70% of asset managers fear Brexit fund passport loss, meaning they will not be able to sell their funds freely across the EU. They manage 7 tn pounds of assets and employ around 50000 people."

BREXIT: BAD FOR THE UNITED
KINGDOM, GOOD FOR THE EU?

Obviously those who will continue to push for Brexit must believe it is good for them and presumably for the United Kingdom, even if it means losing Scotland and perhaps Northern Ireland. The City of London will also suffer, but no one can estimate what the damage will be until the terms of exiting are known.

Jacques Delors, who has dedicated much of his life to the European dream both in public office and after retirement through his Paris-based foundation, made the following observation in an interview in 2012 with the *Handelsblatt* newspaper: "If the British cannot support the trend towards more integration in Europe, we can nevertheless remain friends, but on a different basis. I could imagine a form such as a European economic area or a free-trade agreement."

That might be the happiest outcome should Brexit come to pass. The real beneficiaries of Brexit in that case would be the remaining EU members inspired by people of the experience and quality of Jacques Delors and members of the Spinelli Group, which was founded in 2010 as a network of politicians, individuals, writers, and think tanks looking to revive the momentum toward a federalist structure for the EU.

There is also evidence that the attachment of EU member countries to Europe has been strengthened by the UK Brexit vote. This point was reinforced by comments from Carl Bildt.

Obviously those, such as the Spinelli Group, with the foresight to realize the importance of greater integration and an emerging federalist model would be blocked by a United Kingdom working as an EU member to have reforms move in the opposite direction. This is consistent with Prime Minister Margaret Thatcher's famous Bruges speech in 1988 where she said, "We have not successfully rolled back the frontiers of the state in Britain, only to see them re-imposed at a European level with a European super-state exercising a new dominance from Brussels. Certainly we want to see Europe more united and with a greater sense of common purpose. But it must be in a way which preserves the different traditions, parliamentary powers and sense of national pride in one's own country; for these have been the source of Europe's vitality through the centuries."

This could hardly be seen as an endorsement of a federal system however decentralized, especially the preservation of parliamentary powers, meaning full sovereignty, which is incompatible with federalism. She could have added that the elements she wished to see preserved have also been the source of bloody European conflicts throughout the last millennium, including three wars between France and Germany in the 70 years between 1870 and 1939.

In the following pages, consideration is given to some steps that must be taken to realize the collective potential of the EU as a major global player, which it could never be if its members revert to nation-state status. Indeed, Bildt advised the panel at the 2016 World Knowledge Forum that as other major countries grow in economic clout, not even Germany would be in a new G8. Only a united EU could have influence on the global stage.

FORGETTING THE LESSONS OF HISTORY

Skeptics like Professor Grygiel, many of them American, seem blinded by the headlines and glare of current events, failing to place them in a broader historical context. Reviewing the remarkable evolution of Europe since the Second World War, I hope that the long-term success of Europe is inevitable. But as the great American judge Oliver Wendell Holmes once noted, "the mode by which the inevitable comes to pass is effort." European leadership must now make that effort. It is critical not only for Europe, but for the world today.

A strong, unified Europe is also important for the emergence of true multilateralism and the further evolution of globalization. Since the end of the Cold War we have been living in a world dominated by just one superpower: the United States. Fortunately, that superpower has been a very open market and largely, but not entirely, militarily non-aggressive. Sometimes referred to as the "importer of last resort," it continues to run current account deficits opposite many trading partners, especially China.

The American economy has enough strength and resilience to

emerge slowly but with growing confidence from the global financial crisis of 2007–08. To become a companion economic locomotive, Europe must continue to open its markets, eliminate distorting trade subsidies, and undergo substantial structural reforms in labour, services, and manufacturing markets to stimulate European economic growth.

If that does not happen, the United States might use its economic muscle to focus increasingly on bilateral agreements that are becoming a serious impediment to global free trade. That risk looms even larger now that the Doha Development Round of WTO negotiations, launched in 2001 and for many years gripped by inertia, was abandoned in December 2015.

FAILURE TO MEET GLOBAL CHALLENGES

If Europe had successfully moved to a more centralized and coherent federal model of government it could have reached the objective adopted by the EU in 2000 (often referred to as the Lisbon Agenda), which was stated in the Lisbon Declaration (24 March 2000) as follows: "The Union has today set itself a new strategic goal for the next decade: to become the most competitive and dynamic knowledge-based economy in the world, capable of sustainable economic growth with more and better jobs and greater social cohesion."

Well, that failed. A review of progress chaired by the former Dutch Prime Minister Wim Kok reported in 2004 that the strategy had fallen well short of its objectives. The diagnosis of the problems of broad structural reform was good, but implementation of reforms was seriously lacking. Kok's review carried much credibility as he had overseen the continuation and completion of the major Dutch structural reforms originally introduced by his more conservative predecessor, Ruud Lubbers. Kok was also a regular participant in many international conferences, and during our discussions it was apparent to me that he was a talented consensus builder.

I saw evidence of this when Kok invited me and my chef de cabinet, Carolyn Ervin, for dinner at his official residence in The Hague, where he was bringing together business and labour leaders as well as opposition politicians. The purpose was to discuss economic issues, including challenges to job creation and social coherence. Exchanges around the dinner table were friendly and well informed.

As I commented to Carolyn after we left the dinner, for me this was a unique experience. As a minister in the Canadian federal government I could never have imagined such a non-partisan gathering of leaders with different agendas and different policies.

There is much to be said for such civil relations, which enable intellectual and political opponents to better understand competing views. Strengthening such relations between European political leaders will be important in bringing cohesion and stronger integration to the EU in line with the objectives of the Spinelli Group.

GLOBAL BENEFITS OF A STRONG EU

The Lisbon Declaration has been replaced by the Europe 2020 strategy, which has five ambitious objectives related to employment, innovation, education, social inclusion, and climate/energy. The world would benefit greatly from Europe attaining those objectives. Imagine Europe, the United States, Japan, China, and India all trading, exchanging goods, services, and capital, and driving innovation to ever higher plateaus. In their wake, smaller but associated economies would also prosper, giving multilateralism a chance to raise living standards worldwide.

Today only Europe and Japan look able to match the United States in per capita GDP and hence consumer purchasing power. Demographic projections show Japan's population in serious decline, while an expanded Europe could have several times the population of the United States.

The objectives listed above can only be achieved when the peoples of Europe reach a consensus on what kind of legal community they truly wish to be, and so far progress to that end has been in fits and starts. The failure of the Lisbon Agenda, the rejection of the proposed constitution in both French and Dutch referenda, and now the proposed exit of the United Kingdom underscore the difficulty of moving toward a flexible federal structure.

The use of the word *federal* seems to be an anathema for many Europeans. It is worth repeating that with the creation of the European Coal and Steel Community in 1951 the French government declared that it would "provide for the setting up of common foundations for economic development as a first step in the Federation of Europe."

Today there does not appear to be any coordinated and broad-based visionary leadership of the kind that led Europe out of the chaos of the Second World War. Perhaps the Greek crisis, the withdrawal of the United Kingdom from the EU, and continuing economic performance under potential will awaken Europeans to the need for a truly federal-type union with strong central government institutions accompanied by the protection of individual nations' precious linguistic and cultural identities. The genius of federalism is that it can accommodate great diversity in many areas.

CULTURAL IMPERATIVES OF FEDERALISM

What is the way forward? Where is the higher vision to achieve what is imaginable but not yet within reach? I suggest that the answer is to reconcile the various goals of Europeans, what I call the three Ms: minimizing frictions, maximizing synergies, and maintaining sovereignty.

Some believe they can achieve the first two without a dilution of sovereignty. This is not possible. From my Canadian experience with Quebec, however, I know that it is possible to minimize frictions and maximize synergies while maintaining cultures and national identities. In the case of Quebec, the French language, civil law, religion, and culture have been protected since the Quebec Act of 1774, which is one reason why separatist movements have never succeeded.

I see this kind of flexible federal structure, with necessary variations, in Europe's future. Loss of Europe's various languages and cultures would alter the character of the continent, moving it in the direction of the United States. The historical evolution and the nature of the "self-willed" peoples of Europe make that path neither feasible nor desirable.

REPRESENTATIVE GOVERNMENT –
ITS DENIAL THROUGH REFERENDA

Why are politicians increasingly inclined to duck their responsibilities as representatives of the people? Failure to make progress on reforms must lie squarely on the shoulders of European politicians. Leadership is not exercised through popular referenda. Putting difficult constitutional and technical questions to a vote by the general populace is not an exercise in representative government, as rational decision making risks being overtaken by demagogues and irrational passion. Such factors seemed to have governed the outcome of the Dutch and French referenda and more recently the UK Brexit experience.

Just before the UK referendum, *New Scientist* (4 June 2016) published a commentary (p. 16) in which the writers said, "The EU referendum could be the most irrational yet. Uncertainty over consequences, and contradictory economic and political information, mean that voters will be swung even more than usual by feelings and biases that have nothing to do with the issues at stake."

We seem to be forgetting the nature of representative government as expounded by the great Parliamentarian Edmund Burke in the eighteenth century: "It is his [the elected representative's] duty to sacrifice his repose, his pleasures, his satisfactions, to theirs; and above all, ever, and in all cases, to prefer their interest to his own. But his unbiased opinion, his mature judgment, his enlightened conscience, he ought not to sacrifice to you, to any man, or to any set of men living ... Your representative owes you, not his industry only, but his judgment; and he betrays, instead of serving you, if he sacrifices it to your opinion."

Prime Minister Cameron betrayed his voters to satisfy dissent within the Conservative Party and the long-term consequences for the United Kingdom and its people may be very negative, depending upon the terms of separation. It is hard to believe that the United Kingdom, with a population of about 63 million, can walk away from a remaining market of about 446 million without serious consequence.

Europe must address incoherent political positions on issues that include the absence of an EU-wide stock exchange supported by a regulatory body equivalent to the US Securities and Exchange Commission, the lack of an EU-wide food and drug agency, and the fact that while the free movement of people is guaranteed there is no common immigration and asylum policy. A strengthened EU-wide financial system must be complemented with an equitable equalization formula for the weaker regions whose exports may be threatened when the euro is strong. Such issues should be addressed by elected political leaders, not by the sometimes irrational, ill-informed, and volatile will of the people, as the UK Brexit vote clearly illustrates.

A challenge for Europe is to welcome both foreign investment and commercial ownership and foreigners themselves. Immigration is the only way to halt the demographic decline underway in all European countries, particularly in Italy, Germany, and Spain. As many have observed, the influx of Syrian and other immigrants from wartorn regions should be seen as a partial but important answer to this demographic decline, provided that complementary integration programs are sensible and properly managed.

In today's world, human capital is the most important ingredient of economic success, which translates into greater wealth and rising standards of living for all. Migrants are Europe's future and should be welcomed, educated, and integrated, not alienated from the society they have elected to join. By comparison, debate over foreign economic ownership is trivial. It is sad to meet young Muslims, born and raised in France, who feel excluded from French society. That must change. Europe should look to the strong human capital advantage of the United States, Canada, and Australia, where the vast majority of citizens have identifiable immigrant origins.

TURKEY – UNFORTUNATE AND DANGEROUS EXCLUSION

Europe should have sought a closer alliance with Turkey after President Recep Tayyip Erdoğan brought his Justice and Development Party (AKP) to power in 2002. Immediate reforms quickly transformed the underperforming Turkish economy. One of few countries with a young population and high birth rates, Turkey had much to offer Europe both demographically and strategically. This coincidence of interests suggests that the EU should have welcomed Turkey's membership instead of deferring it.

In numerous meetings I found Erdoğan to be very effective. He seemed well informed on a broad range of subjects. At a meeting in İzmir when President Erdoğan and I lunched with Steve Ballmer of Microsoft, Erdoğan seemed knowledgeable about a range of information and communication issues and made very pertinent comments.

He had a commanding presence and continued to enjoy broad popularity despite lingering suspicions among many that he held Islamic fundamentalist beliefs. Events in 2016 and the resulting turmoil in Turkey suggest that those suspicions may have been right.

When Erdoğan visited me in Paris, we discussed membership in the EU, which seemed clearly to be his ambition, but the EU did not rush to embrace Turkey, which was a mistake. He commented to me during a lunch at my Paris residence that if Europe would not accept Turkey as a member then perhaps the North American Free Trade Agreement would. I thought the comment was in jest, but perhaps not.

Here again, politicians used referenda to thwart the right policy. President Chirac said that he would welcome Turkey as an EU member, but of course, it would have to be approved by a referendum. With the mounting concern of the public and media about Islamic immigrants in the French population, what was the likelihood of a positive outcome of such a referendum?

Erdoğan and his AKP team were well prepared to assume power and carry out ambitious economic reform plans largely under the capable direction of the US-educated Ali Babacan. The first prime minister, Abdullah Gül, was a place card pending the lifting of a ban that kept Erdoğan from assuming that office, which he did after a number of months. Gül then became deputy prime minister, before becoming president in 2007.

I enjoyed working with both of them and greatly admired the speed with which the economy was turned around despite difficult reforms, yet with the AKP party retaining broad-based popularity.

Gül's role as president was a largely ceremonial post until he was replaced by Erdoğan in 2014, who then moved to strengthen the role of the presidency as Putin had done in Russia.

Uneasy relations between the UN, the United States, Russia, and Turkey, frayed by the Syrian conflict, and then the harsh crackdown following the failed 2016 coup, mean that membership in the EU for Turkey now seems unlikely in the foreseeable future despite the obvious benefits for all parties. Despite Babacan's acknowledged competence, he was required to step down from ministerial roles but continues to sit as a member of the legislature. Unfortunately, Erdoğan is increasingly seen as autocratic and anti-secular.

I hope that Turkey, a critical regional and global player and a member of NATO, will preserve and strengthen its democratic institutions. My fear, however, is that its future is uncertain. The EU's refusal to accept Turkey as a member has probably not helped: it is a sad example of not "seizing the moment." Had Europe brought Turkey into the EU, it is conceivable that President Erdoğan would have continued to keep his anti-secularism to himself.

4

Russia: An Opportunity Bungled

During the crisis in the Ukraine the Canadian prime minister observed, "It's increasingly apparent to me that the Cold War has never left Vladimir Putin's mind." That may be true. This view is certainly widely echoed in the international media, with some claiming that Putin wants to recreate the Soviet Union of his youth. Acquiring Crimea and supporting the rebels in east Ukraine are perceived as steps in that direction.

It is clear that Putin's personal agenda is totally incompatible with democratic ideals, free markets, freedom of expression, and even human rights. His popularity is founded on hostility and aggressive policies toward the West.

The disappearance of political adversaries, be they politicians or journalists, carries serious implications for the future of any semblance of a Russian democracy rooted in the rule of law. The brutal assassination of the talented and charismatic opposition leader Boris Nemtsov, whom I met with in Moscow when he was a deputy prime minister, points to intimidation of a kind we associate with ruthless dictatorial regimes.

Putin did not have to happen. Until Boris Yeltsin appointed him prime minister in 1999 the name *Putin* seldom surfaced in the consideration of Russian affairs. In fact it was widely thought that Yevgeny Primakov might be the next president. However, that did not happen, probably for the reason mentioned in Primakov's obituary in the *Economist* (15 July 2015): "When he [Primakov] said he would empty the jails to make room for Russia's business elite, Mr Yeltsin sided with the oligarchs and publicly disparaged him as 'useful, for now.' His chances of the presidency vanished in a few days."

Putin is a product of Western blindness to the historic opportunity presented by the collapse of the Soviet Union, something people of my generation dreamt of as we grew up in the post-war shadow of nuclear annihilation under the policy of MAD (mutually assured destruction).

COLD WAR WARRIORS

From my perspective, acquired as secretary-general of the OECD with extensive exposure to senior Russian leaders, Putin and other Russians of similar persuasion believe that the West also harbours many Cold War warriors in positions of influence. Is that why so little effort was made to help move Russia into the mainstream of democratic market economies in the early 1990s?

It is tragic that the Western powers did not move quickly at the most senior political levels to seize the moment and help Russia transition to a market economy as they had with Poland and other Central European nations escaping communist regimes. This should have been a priority in the early 1990s, before Putin walked on the Russian political stage.

THE WEST BLOWS IT

The chance to change the course of history was forgone. Upon my arrival at the OECD at the end of May 1996, my predecessor, Jean-Claude Paye, had just received a request from then-Prime Minister Viktor Chernomyrdin for Russia to join the OECD.

Becoming a member is not an easy procedure, and I was left to follow it up throughout my ten-year tenure as secretary-general. I started the process with an official visit to Moscow in October 1997. I took a large team from the OECD, experts in the major policy areas that should have been Russian priorities as the government sought to launch membership negotiations with the organization.

What a contrast with the Moscow I had visited with an official delegation in 1983 when I was a minister in the Canadian federal cabinet of Pierre Trudeau. Even the visible changes in Moscow were striking, with billboards promoting Western products, from shoes to Marlboro cigarettes to McDonalds with its golden arches, on every major thoroughfare. Compared with the drab Moscow I recalled, with its oppressive communist atmosphere, little traffic, and a lane on each major artery reserved for politicians, senior officials, and visiting dignitaries, this seemed a different place. Only my large, dark suite in the President Hotel, where the government lodged many official visitors, was reminiscent of Soviet days.

My view over the Moskva River was marred by a monstrously ugly statue nearly 100 metres high erected as a tribute to Peter the Great. Commissioned by Moscow Mayor Yuri Luzhkov, the statue had just been completed. It was, and remains, very controversial. Muscovites find it hideous and wonder why they should pay tribute to Peter the Great, who moved the capital from Moscow to St. Petersburg.

Ugly as it is, I wondered whether it would eventually be seen as a symbol of Moscow just as the Eiffel Tower, now seen as the symbol of Paris, was initially very controversial and was slated for demolition in the early years of the twentieth century. Today, apartments are promoted as having a view of the Eiffel Tower. Does the same happy fate await Peter the Great's statue?

During that decade I met with many enthusiastic Russian reformers, including prime ministers, notably Mikhail Kasyanov, deputy prime ministers, the accomplished Finance Minister and Deputy Prime Minister Alexei Kudrin, and a host of other politicians and officials.

Many, including Kudrin, dined at my official residence in Paris, sometimes gathering around my piano to sing nostalgic Russian ballads. Before their visits I practised playing the music from a CD of Russian melodies. I always found it inspiring but sad music, and I loved hearing it sung by my Russian friends.

Most of my Russian guests were dedicated reformers, eager to integrate with Europe and the West in general. The exceptions seemed to be Prime Minister Mikhail Fradkov, who continues in the Putin entourage as head of the intelligence service (which replaced the KGB), perhaps Primakov, who died in June 2015, and Igor Shuvalov, the current first deputy prime minister.

Shuvalov, who spoke impeccable English, impressed me as being very Westernized and urbane. It has since been revealed in various press reports that his attachments to the West are perhaps too strong – that his family, with vast wealth, controls an offshore Virgin Islands company owned by his wife and maintains a home in Austria and an apartment in London.

My several meetings with Primakov, first in his role as foreign minister and then later as prime minister, were cordial, informative, and relaxed. During his brief stint as prime minister (1998–99) we met on a wintry day in Moscow. He was accompanied by his first deputy, Yuri Maslyukov, who had been given major economic responsibilities in the wake of the 1998 financial crisis.

I travelled to the meeting from the same President Hotel in a limousine preceded by a police car winding through the slippery streets of blowing snow and heavy traffic, narrowly avoiding collisions. This somewhat harrowing experience made me think that the previous system of a dedicated lane for official cars had its advantages for the privileged few.

Primakov greeted me warmly and I presented him with a bottle of Quebec maple syrup. He in turn inquired about my taste for vodka and advised me that the best Stolichnaya vodka came from a distillery near his home. I did not know that the quality of vodka of the same brand could vary from distillery to distillery. Later that day, as I left my last meeting, I was handed a beautifully wrapped bottle of Stolichnaya, with his compliments.

Despite his efforts to crack down on corruption, was Primakov a reformer and would his policies have been different than those of Putin? Many think not.

UNDERSTANDING PUTIN

Admittedly, President Putin himself was hard to read. Shortly after he succeeded Boris Yeltsin as president, he invited me to meet with him and his minister of the economy, German Gref, during an official visit to Paris at the end of October 2000.

By then I had twice visited with key players in Moscow, and many senior Russian politicians and officials had come to Paris. I had also studied Gref's economic plan so was well prepared for the meeting.

Gref and I engaged in a serious review of economic issues as well as the advantages that association with the OECD could offer. We agreed that the ultimate shared goal would be membership, which was the official position taken by the OECD members in 1996.

With no fanfare, the door behind me opened and President Putin joined the conversation. He was very cordial, and we continued the three-way discussion through translators as it appeared that neither Putin nor Gref spoke English or French.

Putin questioned me at some length about the OECD and its various roles. I focused on the organization's importance to emerging market economies. Russia, I noted, would have access to the best economic development practices of the advanced OECD economies, including the extraordinary achievements of members that had recently joined, such as South Korea.

Regulatory reform, liberalization of trade, effective taxation, privatization, and policies to attract foreign direct investment all figured in our discussion. Putin listened intently, nodding from time to time when a comment seemed particularly relevant to his thinking.

I added that I was beginning to focus not only on best practices but also on bad practices. Every country has its share of the latter, but governments are often slow and politically reluctant to admit to mistakes.

He looked at me impassively and asked, "Do you have some examples?"

Surprised by the question, my thoughts raced over my experience as the Canadian minister at one time responsible for economic and regional development.

"Yes," I replied. "In Canada, which is a vast and diversified country and has similarities with Russia, we committed many mistakes. We pushed local development policies that were more tailored to positive political outcomes than to economic ones."

He nodded but did not follow up, probably recognizing that in democracies, placating local constituencies with public funds is an odious, yet obvious, by-product of the election process.

I sensed that Putin was open to engaging seriously with the OECD to further Russia's economic development and integration in the world economy. Why else would he invite me to explain in some depth (and in the presence of his chief economic architect, German Gref) the benefits that OECD membership could bring to Russia?

But it was soon clear that the reformers pushing for more transparent and co-operative engagement were confronting a reluctant president who was dubious that the West was genuinely interested in Russia's development. The president had good reason for his reluctance, given the hostile Western initiatives that were soon to follow, notably the proposed missile defence system and NATO expansion to the borders of Russia.

Had the West been open to closer relations with Russia sooner, and had the Bush administration refrained from policies of containment, the isolation and lack of mutual trust, as well as the Crimean and Ukrainian crises, might have been avoided. In fact, many of the policy failures outlined in this book might have had much better outcomes had Russia, Europe, and the United States been playing on the same team with common objectives. Think of Syria and the Middle East, the multilateral trade agenda, and the battles against climate change, corruption, and international terrorism as examples.

Syria in particular brought the world closer to a cold war, with Russia supporting the government of Bashar al-Assad and pretending to be fighting ISIS while bombing the rebels supported by the United States. Each government was represented by a capable foreign minister in the persons of Secretary John Kerry and long-serving Russian Foreign Minister Sergey Lavrov. From all appearances they also seemed to have established a good personal relationship, which did not surprise me, as I had met Kerry several times in small groups at Davos and had worked with Lavrov for a time in the liaison committee we had established with Moscow. They were both personable, intelligent, and well informed. The collapse of the ceasefire they had negotiated and the renewal of brutal bombings of Aleppo by Syrian government and Russian aircraft with the killings of countless civilians made me realize that personal relationships had not built the trust necessary to prevent such disasters. We seemed to be on the threshold of a renewed cold war.

During my time at the OECD, some key members of the organization manifested little enthusiasm for the "ultimate shared goal" of Russian membership or rated it a high priority. Some may have been pleased that Russia, a former threatening adversary, was struggling to overcome its economic and social woes during the dismal 1990s before Putin's presidency. Was this "schadenfreude"?

LITTLE HELP, MUCH PROVOCATION

State revenues in Russia were abysmal. Inadequate tax revenues meant that many public servants were underpaid. The untaxed and unmeasured black economy thrived, as did corruption.

A government is only as good as its public service. Despite constant complaints, in most Western democracies we take our good public services for granted. Sure, there are examples of waste, and there is occasional corruption, but it is never systemic as it was, and is, in Russia.

How much did we support Russian reformers attempting to build basic governance infrastructure so that appropriate regulations could be adopted and enforced in all areas, including taxation? Did we help this wonderful country, now freed from the shackles of communism and central planning, to regain its stature as an industrial and cultural giant in the international community of nations?

After neglecting Russia in the early 1990s, it took the OECD another eleven years after Chernomyrdin's request in 1996 to invite Russia to begin the accession process for membership. (It was suspended because of the Crimean situation.)

Had OECD developed countries, led by the United States, helped Russia and Russians to develop a healthy market-oriented and properly regulated economy in the immediate post-Soviet period, Russia might have weathered the economic storm of 1998. Instead, it was brought down by a toxic combination of the global instability flowing from the 1997 Asian financial crisis, a collapse in the price of Russian commodity exports, soaring unemployment, and a loss of foreign investor confidence evidenced by capital outflows. The result was the Russian default of 1998 with a devaluation of the ruble, domestic debt in default, and a moratorium on foreign payments.

Inflation hit 84 per cent. These major economic setbacks further undermined the credibility of the reformers and the importance of open market economies.

Could this have been avoided? Compare the positive experience of post-communist economies that were supported by expert teams from the OECD and the EU through the SIGMA program (Support for Improvement in Governance and Management) with the "shock" treatment applied to Russia. The difference is startling.

Unfortunately, the "Harvard boys" got to Russia before the OECD did. Their advice on economic restructuring and privatization resulted in the transfer of much Russian public wealth to a handful of oligarchs. The magnitude of that wealth transfer to a few oligarchs is well described in Chrystia Freeland's book *Sale of the Century: Russia's Wild Ride from Communism to Capitalism* (Crown Business, 2000). This experience embittered average Russians, who understandably did not, and do not, perceive Western-style capitalism as being in their interest.

Putin has so far been the beneficiary of that anger. His popularity is buoyed by his obvious antipathy toward and distrust of the West, especially the United States.

Just before leaving the OECD in 2006 I expressed my frustration and alarm at our relations with Russia. In a letter to the 30 member countries on 5 April 2006, I sent a lengthy and detailed plea for a change in attitude toward Russia. Here are limited excerpts:

Dear Ambassadors:

I have just returned from Russia for the last time as Secretary-General of the OECD.

As I prepare to step down from my role as Secretary-General I would like to share with you my profound disappointment and concern about the future of Russia and this Organization. Indeed, we have had the opportunity to make a solid contribution to the future of Russia as a strong democratic country with a market oriented economy which we risk forfeiting for reasons which border on the trivial in the great scheme of things ... looking at the present in light of the past is useful.

The present which I have again witnessed first-hand might be characterized as a struggle between reformers and those who still cling to the vestiges of a Soviet style command control economy ... [P]rogress [on reform] is slow and painful and always runs the risk of slipping backwards with who knows what consequences ... Ten years ago when Russia formally applied for membership I was optimistic that it would happen before I left the Organization. I saw this as one of the most important reform anchors that Russia could have. It was climbing a steep treacherous rock face and the OECD was poised to hand it a rope to help guide it to the summit. Never would Russia again slip into the mould of an alienated dictatorship armed with the nuclear capacity to hold the western world to ransom and put the extraordinary planetary benefits of globalization into reverse ... There is no excuse to delay launching an invitation to commence the accession process.

Because of this unique position that Russia enjoys, the OECD has an historic opportunity to reach out to Russia, engage Russia and ensure that history applauds the important role of the OECD rather than denigrating it for letting petty issues get in the way of serious global progress towards peace, security and prosperity.

Donald Johnston,
Secretary-General of the OECD

During the ten years following Chernomyrdin's request, Western countries should have been doing everything in their power to build mutual trust and bring Russia into the grand community of democratic nations. Instead, they were trying to contain Russia.

Encouraging the Ukraine to join the EU and US-led NATO and proposing to put missiles into Poland on the fiction that they were intended to shield Europe and Russia from Iranian missile attacks were widely recognized as ill-conceived and provocative steps. Hardly worthy of a sophisticated US foreign affairs department, they corroborated Putin's view that the West remains an enemy not to be trusted.

It is obvious that repairing the relationship with Russia is urgent. Is this possible with Putin in power?

While he may be popular with the people, his outspoken critics seem seriously committed to reform. Can we support them without feeding the widespread anti-West sentiments that Putin has nurtured?

I have referred above to some politicians I felt were reformists. It is courageous to be an outspoken critic of the Kremlin today, as evidenced by the assassination of Boris Nemtsov and journalists. But there remain some willing to speak out.

A good example is economist Andrei Illarionov, whom I knew as the president's chief economic adviser; I met with him numerous times both at Davos and in the Kremlin. In December 2005 he resigned from his position as President Putin's representative to the G8. At the time he declared, "This year Russia has become a different country. It is no longer a democratic country. It is no longer a free country."

He has continued his outspoken criticism from his base in Washington.

Is the international community's isolation of Russia and the imposition of more sanctions likely to undermine Putin's leadership or have the opposite effect? Even if Russia were invited back into the G8, would Putin agree to participate? Is the pursuit of OECD membership even realistic given the deterioration of relationships and the escalation of sanctions?

History demonstrates that engagement and economic interdependence, even between former enemies, is the road to peace. There is no better example than the Europe of today, forged in large measure by the Marshall Plan.

The mutual engagement and interdependence created within the EU after 1945 makes wars between members unthinkable. Today, countries lob criticism and insults instead of bombs and bullets. That is progress, I judge, and Russia should and could have been part of that community. The West blew it, and the long-term consequences could be tragic unless a genuine reset button can be quickly found. That seems unlikely.

Russia is probably heading for an economic meltdown into a deep recession and yet another default unless Putin reverses course and rapidly brings the Ukraine adventure to a peaceful conclusion. The political beneficiary of the 1998 default, would Putin survive an economic collapse largely of his own making? Remember the fall of Nikita Khrushchev in October1964 after ten years of political domination? William Tompson noted in his study of Khrushchev's fall (*Khrushchev: A Political Life*, Palgrave Macmillan, 1995) that "he was stripped of his party and state posts and sent into an obscure retirement by the very men who had been closest to him throughout his long career."

A similar fate might befall Putin if his policies destroy the wealth of oligarchs and drive the country into economic deprivation. The reformers might then return to positions of influence. If so, the West must not again let them down.

This failure to support Russia at a critical time was well documented by economist Jeffrey Sachs in 2012. He was engaged with a number of countries such as Poland, which served as an example for a successful transition from a centralized communist regime to a market economy. Having been criticized for the Russian failure, he wrote the following blog post (at jeffsachs.org) on 14 March 2012:

> In December 1991 I had continuing discussions with the IMF about Western assistance for Russia. The IMF's point man, John Odling-Smee, who lasted for a decade as the head of the IMF's efforts, was busy telling the G-7 that Russia needed no aid, that the "balance of payments gap" as calculated by the IMF was essentially zero. I believe that the IMF was simply parroting the political decisions already decided by the United States, rather than making an independent assessment. This is just a conjecture, but I make it because of the very low quality of IMF analysis and deliberations. They seemed to be driving towards conclusions irrespective of the evidence. The IMF's approach was in any event just what the rich countries wanted to hear. The technical methodology was primitive beyond belief.

I have spent time here and there with Sachs, whom I admire, and while I have not always been in agreement with him from the political economy point of view, I think he is spot on in his criticism of the West in this context. We failed Russia, but more importantly we failed the Russian people. It may turn out to be one of the great tragedies of history. Going through notes I made after my 1997 visit, I found this aspirational paragraph:

> Imagine a Russia with strong investment protection legislation and regulation: the rule of law rigorously applied; well-defined and fairly applied competition policy; a judicial system functioning efficiently and honestly beyond the reach of any political influence; high standard democratic practices; an investment policy that attracts businesses to Russia's massive natural resources and its human resources – the best and the brightest! What an opportunity for Russia, for long-term security in the Euro Atlantic Region and for the world.

Sadly it was not to be, and Western powers bear much responsibility for Putin's Russia.

5

Statistics: Their Uses and Abuses

There are three kinds of lies: lies, damned lies, and statistics.

Mark Twain

Inundated with competing statistics about every aspect of our lives, how do we distinguish between good and bad information? This is a relevant question for everyone and vital for economists, politicians, public servants, and businesses who rely upon statistics to formulate knowledge-based policies. Accurate, up-to-date, and comparable statistics are critical for public policy development and of enormous importance for businesses across the planet in this rapidly globalizing world. National statistical agencies must supply the OECD and other agencies with reliable, accurate, and comparable statistics that allow them to track the progress of the world's diverse societies and economies. It was clear to me as secretary-general that establishing reliable global statistical standards for all countries is a never-ending process and one of the OECD's most important functions, given its depth of expertise and professional objectivity.

ACCURACY CRITICAL –
VIEW FROM WASHINGTON EXPERTS

The importance of the OECD's work in this area was brought home to me during one of my first official visits to Washington, in early October 1996, an exploratory trip only months after I became secretary-general. I was fortunate to be accompanied by one newly named deputy secretary-general, Joanna Shelton, a former deputy assistant secretary for trade policy at the US State Department.

She quickly became a wonderful asset, taking over at different times difficult files such as corporate governance, regulatory reform, and much of our initial work on information and communication technology. My colleagues and I were disappointed and saddened in 1999 when she and her husband, Dick Erb, a former number two at the IMF, decided to abandon Paris for a ranch in Montana. She was a great loss.

The State Department had prepared a good but crowded program. It included meetings with Commerce Secretary Mickey Kantor; Under Secretary of State Joan Spero; Assistant Secretary of State Al Larson; National Economic Council member Dan Tarullo (who recently resigned from the Federal Reserve Board); Joe Stiglitz, then chair of the Council of Economic Advisers, and members Alicia Munnell and Jeff Frankel; the head of USAID, Brian Atwood; US Trade Representative Charlene Barshevsky; Alan Greenspan, chair of the Federal Reserve Board; Secretary of Labor Robert Reich; White House National Economic Adviser Laura D'Andrea Tyson; and finally Attorney General Janet Reno.

What an introduction to such official visits! It was demanding, even exhausting, but a wonderful learning experience for a new secretary-general of the OECD. It was helpful that Joanna Shelton knew many of the participants and was obviously much appreciated by our interlocutors.

I looked forward to meeting Laura Tyson again because of my faux pas the previous year when she was the chair of the Council of Economic Advisers to the President and I was campaigning for the post of secretary-general. The Canadian Department of Foreign Affairs had provided me with a briefing book on each person I was scheduled to meet on the campaign. I carefully read each one. The brief on Laura Tyson said she received a PhD in 1961 so I assumed she would be about my age, as I graduated in law in 1958. The briefing book did not provide me with a picture.

When I was ushered into the office of the Chair of the Council of Economic Advisers in the Executive Office Building of the White House I was greeted by this very attractive young woman in a red blazer whom I assumed was an assistant. After a warm handshake I said I was here to meet Laura Tyson, the chair of the council.

Raising an eyebrow and looking puzzled, she said, "That's me."

After that awkward introduction we went on to have a useful discussion about the OECD because in her role at the council she had chaired the Economic Policy Committee in Paris, as had Alan Greenspan, who had also been the chair of the council some years before.

I met Laura Tyson again years later when we both participated in an economic discussion in London at the Queen Elizabeth Conference Centre under the chairmanship of the deputy governor of the Bank of England, Mervyn King. She was then dean of the London Business School. We all waited patiently for John Snow, secretary of the US Treasury, to join the conversation from his Washington office through the speakerphone system for all to hear. Chairman King then advised us that Snow's car was stuck in a snowstorm, which received a good laugh from the assembled experts.

At almost every meeting during that first visit to Washington, emphasis was placed upon the importance of OECD statistics. While the OECD cannot develop the raw data, it sets standards that give credibility to the data and ensures that they are comparable among member governments. In addition it can suggest new statistical series that can be of benefit to policy-makers.

In this first tour of Washington the OECD role in statistics was a principal focus of my discussions with Joe Stiglitz, Laura Tyson, Dan Tarullo, and Alan Greenspan. Specifically, Stiglitz was concerned about discrepancies between productivity-measured increases and those of economic growth. He emphasized the importance of developing standards to facilitate comparative analyses across countries. Alan Greenspan picked up on the same point, saying, "If we're concerned about productivity and prices, and we know that the numbers must be wrong, if would be helpful to correct our misunderstandings."

Charlene Barshevsky had an impressive grasp of complex trade issues and was enthusiastic about the prospects for economic growth and development that multilateral free trade promised. While praising the quality of OECD's work, she also was harshly critical of the timing of the release of the OECD publication *Open Market Matters*. She claimed that it came out too late to play an effective role in reinforcing the debates in parliaments and the US Congress for those seeking to defeat protectionism in its many forms in different countries.

This was an important message for OECD experts. We were not like other economic think tanks because the OECD's work was commissioned by and supported the policy options of senior policy-makers in capitals. This was a message that would influence my team's thinking about the importance of the timeliness of the OECD's work. Being a lawyer, I saw the experience Barchevsky described as analogous to handing a litigator a brilliant brief in the courtroom just after the legal arguments had closed. Joanna and I left Washington thinking how much work we needed to do but also how valuable it was to listen carefully and respond quickly to the concerns of client governments.

In 2001 I recruited a new chief statistician, Italian Enrico Giovannini. He was eager to reinforce the international role that Stiglitz, Barshevsky, and Greenspan had mentioned and to look at a new social development statistical series that went beyond the widely accepted GDP numbers that most economists embraced as a measure of a country's progress.

My keen interest in this area was stimulated by an unexpected event. In early 1996, when I was the secretary-general designate, I attended a Stockholm conference of women leaders from across the globe.

GDP – SACROSANCT BUT LIMITED

During an economic discussion chaired by Maria Livanos Cattaui, then president of the International Chamber of Commerce, Cattaui expressed her strongly held views on the importance of open market economies and extolled the economic performance of some Asian Tigers. Suddenly a young woman leapt to her feet in protest and cried out, "We are told that our country is developing at a remarkable rate, with GDP growth of 8 per cent, but is this progress when we cannot drink the water, we breathe polluted air, there is raw sewage in the gutters, and our streets are not safe?"

Her spontaneous and passionate intervention had a profound and lasting effect on my own thinking about measuring economic and social progress. GDP is a useful yardstick for some purposes, especially in the developed countries of the OECD where economic growth roughly (but only) tracks improvements in the quality of life of the general population. But today our societies expect and deserve a more comprehensive understanding and measurement of progress. We needed to refine our indicators to express what is important to basic social progress.

This challenge was well captured by the late Robert Kennedy when he discussed the impressive American GDP in the 1960s. In a speech at the University of Kansas in March 1968, he said, "Gross national product counts air pollution and cigarette advertising, and ambulances to clear our highways of carnage. It counts special locks for our doors and the jails for the people who break them. It counts the destruction of the redwood and the loss of our natural wonder in chaotic sprawl. It counts napalm and counts nuclear warheads and armored cars for the police to fight the riots in our cities ... Yet the gross national product does not capture the health of our children, the quality of their education or the joy of their play ... it measures everything, in short, except that which makes life worthwhile."

Understanding that the concept of growth must include the progress of our society as a whole, former French President Nicolas Sarkozy commissioned a study led by Nobel laureate Joe Stiglitz to look specifically at this challenge. Enrico Giovannini was ahead of the curve and with his OECD team was a major contributor to Stiglitz's work.

Before Sarkozy's initiative I had participated in gatherings focused on the subject in Palermo, Bellagio, and Istanbul.

OECD's Statistics Directorate, currently led by Martine Durand, continues to gather up-to-date, accurate, and nationally comparable data on well-being. This very important initiative is readily accessible to all on the OECD website.

Statistics are information, but information is not knowledge, as Einstein famously observed. Statistics are the raw building blocks of knowledge, just as steel is the raw material for the manufacture of automobiles. In the next step, knowledge turns steel into cars and converts raw statistics into relevant information used to formulate policy. Giovannini wisely entitled the first major OECD conference on the subject, held in Palermo's beautiful opera house, Statistics, Knowledge, Policy.

STATISTICS, KNOWLEDGE, POLICY

Here is a specific illustration of this approach. Some economists accept the concept of NAIRU, the non-accelerating inflation rate of unemployment. The theoretical underpinning of this formulation is that when unemployment declines to a certain level, the pool of available labour shrinks and workers have more leverage to obtain wage increases, putting upward pressure on inflation. This theory illustrates the paradigm we are discussing here, that statistics contribute to knowledge and in turn to policy.

It begins with data on inflation and the level of unemployment. This is the raw material for developing knowledge about the relationship between them: the NAIRU. As unemployment falls, central bankers will provide a policy response – usually a tightening of monetary policy to control anticipated inflation – when they believe the NAIRU is being reached. Though policy responses will vary from country to country it is essential to ensure the quality of the statistics from which knowledge is derived. If the unemployment or inflation numbers are wrong, the knowledge will be flawed and the policy response inappropriate.

During the 2007–08 global financial crisis, if the Federal Reserve Board under Ben Bernanke had adhered religiously to this formula (which gratefully it did not), there might have been less liquidity and weaker stimulus programs, and the recession would probably have been longer and deeper. The appropriate policy response is another debate, but NAIRU illustrates the importance of reliable statistics when key economic players like central banks make fundamental decisions.

To quote from Joel Best's book *Damned Lies and Statistics* (University of California Press, 2012): "While some social problems statistics are deliberate deceptions, many – probably the great majority – of bad statistics are the result of confusion, incompetence, innumeracy, or selective self-righteous efforts to produce numbers that reaffirm principles and interests that their advocates consider just and right."

Best points a finger at the fundamental problem of bias. There is a famous quote from an anonymous lawyer who declared before a court: "I will base my facts on the following conclusions."

It is important that we examine statistics with a critical eye to assess their source, quality, and purpose. But the general public, without the ability, time, or interest to do so, will absorb and repeat the numbers that cater to their preconceived opinions. The media has a central role to play and too often it does not play it very well.

ASSESSING THE VALIDITY OF PUBLISHED STATISTICS

Published statistics seem to acquire a life of their own even if their source is close to a guesstimate. We also face a problem that Best describes as mutant statistics: numbers that mutate as they are repeated. He cites an amusing example to illustrate the point. Serving on a student's dissertation committee, he read this sentence in the student's thesis: "Every year since 1950, the number of American children gunned down has doubled." He checked the journal from which the statistic was taken and indeed found the same sentence. He then calculated that the compounding element of doubling every year brought the number of children gunned down in 1995 to well over the total population of the United States.

The author of this remarkable statement claimed to have obtained it from the Children's Defense Fund yearbook of 1994, where the following was said: "The number of children killed each year by guns has doubled since 1950." Since the population had increased by 73 per cent over the same period, the number was not a stunning surprise. The subtle change of wording in the journal article cited by the student was probably accepted by many without question.

This digression underscores the need to objectively analyze statistics that risk the propagation of false information. Education systems should teach our youth to carefully assess the validity of the masses of data they will encounter in today's world of statistical wars. Because public policy based on bad information through flawed statistics will inevitably fail, it is critical that we reach consensus on the methodology underlying statistics with global implications.

Politicians, economists, and business leaders must have accurate and timely data from the 19 countries plus the EU that together make up the G20. These economies represent about 85 per cent of total world output, 80 per cent of world trade, and two-thirds of the world population. Accomplishing that objective will take much time and investment, especially in countries where expertise is lacking. International co-operation offered by the World Bank and the OECD can help countries that lack expertise and resources to improve and monitor the quality of their statistics.

Even the measurement of economic growth has become more complex in recent years: the development of services, the broad introduction of information and communication technologies, the continuous creation of new products, the globalization of production processes, and the increasing role of various financial instruments have all made GDP growth more difficult to measure.

MEASURING THE UNDERGROUND ECONOMY

The non-observed, underground or black economy is especially difficult to measure, but in some countries, even within the G20, it is estimated to be large enough to undermine the credibility of GDP numbers and influence policy responses. Statistics in these immeasurable areas are really intelligent estimates at best.

Bloomberg Business News (30 January 2014) states:

Spain's black economy has flourished as the country struggled through a brutal economic downturn. A new study released by the Finance Ministry estimates off-the-books activity accounted for 24.6 percent of Spain's economy at the end of 2012, up from 17.8 percent before the crisis began in 2008. Spain's shadow-economy problem is now one of the worst in Western Europe. A report last year pegged Greece's black economy at 24 percent of GDP, Italy's at 21 percent, and Spain's at 19 percent. Still another report from 2013 estimated that 1 million Spaniards work off-the-books. The existence of a "high, persistent, and permanent level" of underground unemployment helps explain why Spain's official jobless rate remains at a stubbornly high 26 percent, even as economic recovery takes hold.

Is more information improving decision making, governance, business strategies, and standards of living? We are overwhelmed by the record volume of statistics inundating us via television, print, and the Internet. Politicians insert figures into every speech. Businesses use micro and macro data to make decisions about investments and future production. Non-governmental organizations (NGOs) parade statistics in front of the public every day to support their cause of choice. How reliable are these statistics and how can we know what information we should pay attention to?

In the early 1980s we spoke of the information society. Now we speak of knowledge-based societies. More information does not necessarily ensure better decision making or policy development. In today's economy, knowledge has become the most important factor of production and the most important kind of human capital. But it must be founded on reliable statistics and information. For example, as a knowledge-building organization, the OECD develops useful statistical series and collects and disseminates these basic raw materials of knowledge to the global community.

The well-known Programme for International Student Assessment (PISA), which the OECD launched in 2000, measures on a comparable basis the performance of students and of school systems across the membership. The PISA results encourage countries to analyze their education systems in light of better education outcomes elsewhere. The results have also stimulated public awareness about the quality of their students, teachers, and schools.

This example demonstrates how a serious research program, backed by relevant and reliable statistical information, can mobilize resources, increase the quality of policy debate, help countries develop strategies to address key challenges, and improve the public's understanding of the economic and social challenges they face. In short, it facilitates the chain Statistics, Knowledge, Policy.

NEW CHALLENGES DEMAND ACCURATE STATISTICS

Apart from the statistics that have been gathered by national and international bodies for decades, the world faces new challenges that require accurate data from which knowledge can be derived and upon which policy responses can be developed. Consider climate change, where massive amounts of data are being gathered on the state of the biosphere's natural capital, namely, the soil, the water, the atmosphere, and biodiversity. The knowledge derived from such data, which must be accurate and verifiable, has enormous public policy implications for the well-being of life on this planet.

6

The Economists and the Dismal Science

Economists are enjoying unprecedented prominence these days and many have built high public profiles. Journalists seem fascinated by their predictions and analysis. No matter how often economists get it wrong, print and broadcast media still listen and publish their nostrums.

During my tenure at the OECD and in the years that followed I have worked with and observed many prominent economists. It would be difficult to follow a career as an economist anywhere without using OECD statistics and studies or participating in OECD work, and often both.

CONSENSUS THROUGH COMMITTEE WORK

Of the many committees at the OECD that focus on various aspects of economic policy there were two in particular that brought key economic experts to Paris on a regular basis: the Economic Policy Committee (EPC) and Working Party 3 (WP3).

EPC was created in 1961 at the founding of the OECD with the following mandate: (1) the Economic Policy Committee will keep under review the economic and financial situation and policies of Member countries with a view to attaining the objectives of the Convention; and (2) in reviewing the economic policy of Member countries, the Committee will pay special attention to the international effects of national policies in the light of the increasing interdependence of their economies and of the recognition that efforts of individual countries will be influenced by the actions of others, with a view to establishing a climate of mutual understanding conducive to the harmonious adjustment of policies.

A WHO'S WHO OF OUTSTANDING ECONOMISTS

EPC was traditionally presided over by the chair of the Council of Economic Advisers to the President of the United States. In my time it was chaired by Joe Stiglitz, then by Janet Yellen and Martin Baily, all of whom were named by the Clinton administration. The Bush administration appointed Glenn Hubbard, then Gregory Mankiw.

Each of these people were first-class economists. Stiglitz won the Nobel Prize, Janet Yellen is now chair of the US Federal Reserve Board, and Mankiw and Hubbard are distinguished professors at Harvard and Columbia, respectively. All of them were a delight to work with and each brought different skills and perspectives.

There was wide acclaim when Janet Yellen was named chair of the Federal Reserve. She struck me as thoughtful, reflective, and modest. The Fed chair's importance to the international economic order cannot be exaggerated and Yellen's presence was very welcome. Presumably Stanley Fischer – an academic economist, a central banker, and a former deputy managing director of the IMF – agreed to serve as Yellen's vice chair because of the qualities and experience she brings to the Federal Reserve. (I have the distinction of having taken two chairs of the Federal Reserve, Alan Greenspan and Janet Yellen, to the French Open tennis tournament at Roland Garros.)

WP3 was especially interesting. With only a limited number of participants from the major economic regions, there was time to engage in lively and well-informed debates on policies to promote global economic growth, with a particular focus on three major economic regions: the United States, Europe, and Japan.

When I arrived at the OECD, Larry Summers, then deputy secretary of the US Treasury, chaired WP3. His successors were Mario Draghi, director general, Ministero del Tesoro, Italy; Mervyn King, deputy governor, Bank of England; John Taylor, under secretary of the US

Treasury; and Lorenzo Bini Smaghi, member of the Executive Board, European Central Bank.

They were all excellent chairs and accomplished professionals, with a number moving on to key domestic and international posts. King became governor of the Bank of England and Draghi succeeded Jean-Claude Trichet as head of the European Central Bank.

Bill White, then chief economist at the BIS in Basel, was an important contributor to WP3 meetings, as was the chief economist of the IMF: the brilliant and amusing Michael Mussa, then Ken Rogoff, and finally Raghuram Rajan, whom we knew as Raj, who became governor of the Reserve Bank of India. We also had valuable input from many well-known and capable participants such as Tim Geithner (former secretary of the US Treasury), Mark Carney (governor of the Bank of England), Haruhiko Kuroda (governor of the Bank of Japan), Sir Nigel Wicks, and, on occasion, Sir (now Baron) Andrew Turnbull, both outstanding members of the UK government, and the widely appreciated German state secretary of finance, Caio Koc-Weser.

The OECD's Economics Directorate, led during my time by three outstanding economists (Kumi Shigehara from Japan, Ignazio Visco, later governor of the Bank of Italy, and Jean-Philippe Cotis, who had been the head of forecasting for the French Ministry of Economy and Finance), ensured that the meetings were supported by first-class analytical papers to focus the discussions. Cotis was also a talented amateur magician who frequently entertained our dinner guests, baffling many when coins and playing cards disappeared.

It was stimulating to meet, listen to, and discuss issues with prominent economists at OECD meetings and in other fora such as the annual central bankers' conference in Jackson Hole, Wyoming.

As chair of WP3, after a sleepless overnight flight from the United States Summers would arrive at the OECD and ably chair the meeting sustained only by a can of Coca-Cola that he held with his fingers at the top as if lifting a fragile glass. His duties continued over a working lunch and throughout the afternoon, ending only when dessert plates and coffee cups were removed at the close of a working dinner. Often accompanied by talented staff, Summers was always fully briefed on the papers he had received.

HUBRIS VERSUS ACCURACY

I have met and dealt with many academics, businessmen, bureaucrats, and politicians over the decades. Few could match Summers' intellectual capacity. Though he recognizes his strengths and makes no effort to disguise them, he seems blind to his weaknesses. These have been emphasized by others like the *New York Times*, which severely criticized Summers' policy failures in a transparent effort to derail his ambition to be Ben Bernanke's successor at the Federal Reserve Board. I single out Larry Summers for this critique because he is well known and I think universally recognized as brilliant.

Summers' major weakness, and that of many of his fellow practitioners of the "dismal science" (the term Thomas Carlyle coined for economics in 1749), is that they do not know what they don't know and generally refuse to admit it. This can lead politicians, who have confidence in them, to make serious blunders, sometimes with damaging economic consequences.

Despite their failings, economists have for some years ridden an incredible wave of public interest, even adulation.

MEDIA DARLINGS AND THE NOBEL PRIZE

Every year since 1969, economists have been awarded prizes that are commonly called and publicly accepted as Nobel prizes in economics, which in fact they are not. The Nobel Memorial Prize in Economic Sciences was established in 1968 by the Swedish central bank to honour the memory of Alfred Nobel.

Alfred Nobel established his prize for physics, chemistry, medicine, and literature, and for work in peace. In the media the Nobel economic laureates, as they are often called, seem to eclipse the achievements of "real" scientists who explore new horizons in the natural sciences or the achievements of those in literature or peace.

Obviously in 1895 Nobel knew of great economists such as Stanley Jevons, Alfred Marshall, and Adam Smith who had transformed economies through the promotion of free market economic principles.

But there was no Nobel Prize in economics until 1969. Would Alfred Nobel have agreed? A great grandnephew of Nobel apparently claims this is a misuse of the family name because there never was any intention of establishing a Nobel Prize in economics.

Quite a number of economists actively seek public recognition through the media, which is understandable, except that the media encourages concrete predictions and definitive opinions, which many economists are anxious offer. Carlyle's description of economics as the dismal science still seems appropriate more than 250 years later and many question whether it should be considered a science at all. Some ask how a subject driven by differing ideologies to opposing conclusions can be considered a science.

Chemists, physicists, biologists, and medical doctors frequently admit, "I do not know," or better, "We do not know." How often do we hear a well-known and media-loved economist make such a humble statement? There are notable exceptions, such as Gregory Mankiw commenting in the *New York Times* on 7 May 2011:

After more than a quarter of a century as a professional economist, I have a confession to make: There is a lot I don't know about the economy. In fact, the area of economics where I have devoted most of my energy and attention – the ups and downs of the business cycle – is where I find myself most often confronting important questions without obvious answers. Now if you follow economic commentary in the newspapers or the blogosphere, you have probably not run into many humble economists. By its nature, punditry craves attention, which is easier to attract with certainty, than with equivocation. But that certitude reflects bravado more often than true knowledge.

Bravo!
Secretary of Defense Rumsfeld, hardly noted for humility, said during the Iraq war: "There are things that we know we don't know." Economists would be wise to heed that observation.

In macroeconomics the continuing disagreements between economists on measures to pull economies out of the recession of 2007–08 illustrate the dilemma for policy-makers (e.g., stimulus or tax cuts and austerity measures). The option selected carries profound economic consequences for businesses and individuals.

There is great value in structural or microeconomics where the focus is on the actions and interactions of individuals, businesses, and governments dealing with issues such as labour markets, demographic trends, or the sustainability of pensions. In the United States the National Bureau of Economic Research (NBER), led for thirty years by the remarkable Martin Feldstein and now by James Poterba, has produced many significant and helpful studies and working papers.

FAMOUS ECONOMISTS, INFAMOUS FAILURES

Problems at the micro level sometimes escape the attention of economists, and if they are not identified and dealt with they can migrate to the macro level and have a major impact on the economy as a whole. We witnessed this with the US subprime mortgage derivative crisis, which, thanks to financial engineering and enthusiastic aggressive banking practices, destabilized the entire world economy.

A regional example, which I witnessed first hand, was the Korean credit card crisis of 1999–2000. The government had encouraged the use of credit cards to stimulate spending and help pull the country out of the 1997 economic crisis. It would seem that Koreans splurged on this wondrous plastic and on average held four cards each, running up about $100 billion in collective debt. The avalanche of defaults on credit card payments was large enough to have a negative impact on the national GDP. Although the Korean crisis did not have the same contagious international impact as the subprime derivative problem, it illustrates how quickly bad structural economic mismanagement can translate into a macro problem.

My conclusion is that those focused on macroeconomics often miss fundamental weaknesses in the microeconomy. The subprime crisis and the Korean credit card crisis are obvious examples. Economists did not connect the micro dots.

Econometric modelling, unknown in the pioneering days of economics, certainly has its place, but it will never capture the quirks of human behaviour – individuality, which defies the logical and mathematical outcomes that many economists ascribe to it.

Many prominent economists are given platforms to offer uninformed comments that the media love but that have little basis in the real world. Often their predictions are educated guesses at best, as evidenced by a remarkable lack of consensus among economists on what lies ahead, what actions to take, and the fact that later their recommendations prove to be dead wrong.

Richard Posner has written a good analysis of the 2008 financial crisis in a book entitled *A Failure of Capitalism: The Crisis of 2008 and the Descent into Depression* (Harvard University Press, 2009). I do not agree with the title. In my judgment it is the mismanagement of capitalism, not capitalism itself, that has failed. And do not look to economists to fix it.

A critical review of Posner's book (*Globe and Mail*, 2 May 2009) notes:

> Economists ... tore themselves to public shreds during debate over the past 12 months about what to do. More stimulus or less stimulus? We had prominent economists arguing both sides. Lower interest rates or higher interest rates? Again, economists on either side. Deflation or inflation as the major concern? You guessed it: economists on both sides of the question. The list went on and on, and it became publicly and embarrassingly obvious that economics, outside of a few basic pricing, trade, and profits tenets, has so little consensus as to make astrologers look predictable when it comes to policy prescriptions.

KNOWING WHAT YOU DO NOT KNOW

Too often macroeconomists who do not know what they do not know wrap themselves in ideological clothing, adhering to such nostrums as "the market always self corrects" even in the face of mounting evidence to the contrary. It is worth considering some concrete examples.

Larry Summers, who advised both the Clinton and Obama governments, presided over a small meeting of economists at the Davos Forum in January 2006. This small group of economists were brainstorming on where the economies were headed in the major economic regions: Europe, America, and Japan. In response to my question about the dangers of the housing price bubble in the United States, a problem raised by economists at the OECD, Summers declared that there was no bubble: the issue was strictly a function of supply and demand driven by scarcity in New York City and Boston; there was no problem in Cincinnati. That housing bubble, which for Larry Summers did not exist, began to deflate just months later during the summer of 2006.

In hindsight I was surprised that no one present at this small gathering responded to Summers' confident appraisal of the US housing market. Later one participant was credited with predicting the housing market collapse, which became obvious just six months later. There seemed to be a reluctance to contradict or even argue with Larry Summers. They did not know what they did not know about the housing market in the United States.

Another example is the history of the Harvard economists, known as the Harvard boys, who advised the Russian administration and Anatoly Chubais, an architect of the voucher for shares and loans for shares privatization strategies after the fall of the Berlin Wall. Those actions have been blamed for putting huge parts of lucrative Soviet assets into the hands of a few tycoon oligarchs. As noted economist Jeffrey Sachs has said, "The Russian government not only acted corruptly, not only built up a new oligarchy of billionaires out of nothing, basically, but also gave away its most valuable financial assets – its ownership of the huge natural resource sector in Russia" (interview available at www.pbs.org/wgbh/pages/frontline/shows/crash/interviews/sachs.html).

The actions by favoured apparatchiks and the corruption and dishonesty that allowed valuable state assets to find their way into the hands of a few newly minted billionaires came as a great surprise to those economic counsellors. These measures were not recommendations of Sachs, who had advised Russia in the early 1990s that such natural resource assets remain in the state's hands. Again, they did not know what they did not know about the insatiable greed of these ambitious individuals and the endemic corruption that still beleaguers Russian society.

During a dinner in Moscow a few years ago with a number of young economists and businessmen, I asked them about the privatization that through undue process or skullduggery had led to about 50 per cent of Russia's GDP being placed in the hands of a handful of young oligarchs. There was a frozen silence around the table: the atmosphere that question created was of palpable anger and disgust.

For many reasons Alan Greenspan remains one of my favourite economists, despite the economic meltdown for which so many hold him at least partially accountable. I found his interest in social and economic history and his capacity to place current economic and social issues in an evolutionary context both interesting and impressive.

Greenspan is attacked on several fronts, but there is only one where I see him as vulnerable (and it is not low interest rates): the failure to regulate the derivative market and indeed to resist such regulation, as he subsequently admitted. He was in good democratic company because Robert Rubin and Larry Summers agreed with him.

Greenspan had this to say to the House Committee on Oversight and Government Reform (*New York Times*, 23 October 2008): "Those of us who have looked to the self-interest of lending institutions to protect shareholders' equity, myself included, are in a state of shocked disbelief."

He did not know what he did not know about the short-term greed and motivation of Wall Street.

These observations are not intended to undermine the importance of economics and economists. Economists have a critical role to play, provided they do not stray from their areas of expertise. But too often they do, with scribblers in the media all too anxious to record their latest – often incorrect – predictions.

PREDICTING THE GREAT RECESSION

The recession that began in the United States in December 2007 prompted the greatest economic meltdown since the 1930s. How did this huge body of economic experts within companies, universities, and think tanks, hunkered down each day over computers, sifting through and analyzing data, fail to see this disaster on the horizon?

This remains a mystery, but I hope it has taught a lesson that will bring some humility to practitioners of the dismal science.

Warren Buffett identified derivative instruments, with their growing use, as financial weapons of mass destruction in his annual report of 2002. Who listened?

The economic community, with few exceptions, has confirmed the age-old definition offered by a pundit: "An economist is one who will tell you tomorrow why what he predicted yesterday did not happen today." Very few economists saw the 2008 recession looming despite much empirical evidence of a major bubble. A clip on YouTube shows Peter Schiff of Euro Pacific Capital being questioned by economist Arthur Laffer (of the Laffer curve) and others. They laughed at Schiff's bearish predictions for the months ahead, which turned out to be accurate to an extraordinary degree.

Perhaps too many economists consider themselves the Master Economist as defined by Keynes (*Economic Journal* 34, no. 135 (1924): 311–72):

> The master-economist must possess a rare combination of gifts. He must be mathematician, historian, statesman, philosopher – in some degree. He must understand symbols and speak in words. He must contemplate the particular in terms of the general, and touch abstract and concrete in the same flight of thought. He must study the present in the light of the past for the purposes of the future. No part of man's nature or his institutions must lie entirely outside his regard. He must be purposeful and disinterested in a simultaneous mood; as aloof and incorruptible as an artist, yet sometimes as near the earth as a politician.

This exceptional person exists only in the poetry of Keynes. He may well have considered himself as a prime candidate, and perhaps he was.

The insatiable thirst in the media and among the economics-literate public for the pronouncements and predictions of "economists" is fine and provides good entertainment, but those responsible for public policy must salt their recommendations with heavy doses of scrutiny and healthy skepticism. Had the Russian leadership done that when offered the wisdom of the Harvard boys, the country's economic and social development would probably not be in the sorry state it is today.

BENEFITS FROM ECONOMIC CRISIS

I hope this early twenty-first century global economic crisis will eventually bring concrete benefits. Two come to mind.

First, it has exposed weaknesses in the financial services sector of our market economies where excessive greed and opportunities to satisfy it have placed the foundations of capitalism in jeopardy. Unfortunately, in Western countries, especially in the United States, outsized bonuses in the financial services sector continue to act as a magnet for talent, drawing bright young people who could better serve society in higher callings. I hope that the best and the brightest will now turn to pursuits in the "real economy," with local students taking the empty chairs in our science and engineering classrooms, which have been increasingly filled by foreign students.

Second, economists may finally be humbled, recognizing that in this global economic meltdown most have proven that they do not know what they do not know.

One of the most frustrating aspects of economic expertise for decision makers is the too-frequent absence of consensus on the most serious global challenges. For example, a few years ago, at the conclusion of the China Development Forum in Beijing, participants were invited to a discussion with Premier Wen Jiabao at the Great Hall of the People.

It was an impressive gathering of many prominent economists and a few others, like me, representing international organizations, and major industries with interests in China. Among those present were two Nobel laureates in economics, Robert Mundell and Joe Stiglitz. At the invitation of Sir John Bond, who chaired the session, Mundell opened the discussion with a declaration of strong support for China's controversial monetary policy. He was quickly supported by the other Nobel laureate, Joe Stiglitz.

Their fellow economists, largely American and all with strong professional credentials, were surprised because this was far from a consensus view. Stanley Fischer, a prominent and highly respected economist and now deputy chair of the Federal Reserve, very politely made that point to the Chinese premier. Premier Wen listened attentively. As he left, he thanked us for our wisdom.

What useful advice did Premier Wen take away from that discussion with these prominent economists? Not much. After listening to experts with unequivocal but opposing views, he was left to arrive at his own conclusions and decide the best course of action on China's monetary policy by undoubtedly relying on his own economic advisers.

SAME NUMBERS, DIFFERENT CONCLUSIONS

This situation is well captured in Joe Nocera's comments in the *International Herald Tribune* (2–3 May 2010). Following a series of conferences and workshops in New York where pre-eminent economists offered their views on the Obama administration's response to the economic crisis, Nocera concluded: "Economists and forecasters are looking at the same set of data and coming to radically different conclusions ... sometimes you just have to make up your own mind."

So why did the global financial crisis ignited by the subprime derivative debacle in the United States blindside economic specialists and why have they failed to develop a consensus on solutions? These questions have been asked by millions of people all over the globe, ranging from the man on the street to the Queen of the United Kingdom.

The *Observer* noted on 26 July 2009: "A group of eminent economists has written to the Queen explaining why no one foresaw the timing, extent and severity of the recession. The three-page missive, which blames 'a failure of the collective imagination of many bright people,' was sent after the Queen asked, during a visit to the London School of Economics, why no one had predicted the credit crunch."

Anatole Kaletsky, the principal economic commentator of the *Times of London*, wrote in *Prospect* (April 2009): "The economics profession must bear a lot of the blame for the current crisis. If it is to become useful again it must undergo an intellectual revolution – becoming both broader and more modest."

FINDING FACTS TO SUPPORT CONCLUSIONS

This brings me to another concern, a weakness that I find many of us share to some degree: a tendency to search for facts that support a pre-existing bias or conclusion. I touched on this in the previous chapter.

An example in economics might be the infamous 2010 study by Carmen Reinhart and Ken Rogoff entitled "Growth in a Time of Debt" (NBER Working Paper No. 15639). It argued that high government debt inhibits economic growth and that austerity, not further economic stimulus and debt, was an essential element to restore growth. Their oft-cited conclusion was that excessive public debt (i.e., exceeding 90 per cent of a country's GDP) results in much slower economic growth.

This conclusion was undermined by others who uncovered errors in the study's data, and this was quickly seized upon by Keynesian economists such as Nobel laureate Paul Krugman who held a diametrically opposed view. John Cassidy, writing in the 26 April 2013 issue of the *New Yorker*, sums up the controversy:

> Their most influential claim was that rising levels of government debt are associated with much weaker rates of economic growth, indeed negative ones. In undermining this claim, the attack from Amherst has done enormous damage to Reinhart and Rogoff's credibility, and to the intellectual underpinnings of the austerity policies with which they are associated. In addition, it has created another huge embarrassment for an economics profession that was still suffering from the fallout of the financial crisis and the laissez-faire policies that preceded it. After this new fiasco, how seriously should we take any economist's policy prescriptions,

especially ones that are seized upon by politicians with agendas of their own?

Over the years I have discussed many issues with Ken Rogoff at WP3 where he represented the IMF, at Jackson Hole meetings and more recently during the World Knowledge Forum in Seoul, Korea. He is a brilliant chess player and outstanding economist, and it does not take much exposure to Rogoff to know that you are facing a powerful intellect of many dimensions. I doubt that his reputation will be affected by these events, but they serve as a good lesson for others, specifically, the importance of supporting public policy recommendations with evidence-based facts and not suppositions, which includes setting aside any bias against counterintuitive ideas.

In the extraordinary period of economic turmoil that still dogs us, economists have yet to provide consistent guidance to public policy-makers. Must we follow Joe Nocera's advice and just make up our own minds?

Here is where I believe central bankers and their internal economic advisors have important roles to play so that conflicting economic advice to national leaders does not lead to conflicting policies. Independent central bankers find themselves in a difficult but privileged position. They enjoy substantial public credibility and their status has grown dramatically in recent years. This evolution in their role has not been without controversy; I examine this in the next chapter.

7

Central Bankers and Their Controversies

In the previous pages we saw that economists failed to reach consensus on appropriate policy responses to the economic crisis that drove the world into recession in 2007–08.

Having observed these debates first hand for well over a decade before watching the world economic order reach the verge of collapse in 2007–08, I have come to the view that central bankers and their internal economic advisors have key roles to play in identifying and warning of underlying structural weaknesses in their respective economies. They can ensure that conflicting economic advice to national leaders does not lead to conflicting policies. That is why the regular gathering of central bankers at the Bank of International Settlements' Basel Committee is so important to leaders seeking consensus on key aspects of each other's monetary policies.

One celebrated example was the disagreement between European countries over the Greek bailout proposals. National leaders normally do not have sophisticated economic expertise. They must rely on their "backroom boys" – economic advisers who are often invisible to the public. If their respective economic advisers disagree on policy, clearly the leaders will as well. This fact deserves emphasis because it is not always appreciated by pundits in the media and the general public.

In mid-May 2015 bankers and economists attending a meeting in Sintra, Portugal, listened as the head of the European Central Bank, Mario Draghi, delivered this message (*International New York Times*, 22–23 May 2015, p. 22): "political leaders [in Europe] need to overhaul their chronically underachieving economies ... [and] governments

need to address impediments to investment and growth like bureau-
cracy, legal barriers to hiring and firing, and overregulation."

Larry Summers, who was present at that meeting, seemed to take
issue with Draghi's remarks. "Central banks," he said, "will get themselves in deep trouble if they try to believe they can be major forces
to dismantle what other people consider social protections" (*International New York Times*, 23–24 May 2015, p. 22).

True, if they believe that. They must function independently of the
political process, but I see them as having an important pedagogi-
cal role. Unlike academic economists, who seem to escape objective
evaluation of their predictions and remedies, central bankers' fore-
casts and actions on monetary policy can make, or break, both their
national economies and their own reputations and careers.

For example, the US Congress has mandated the Federal Reserve
System to manage monetary policy so as to achieve maximum
employment, stable prices, and moderate long-term interest rates. In
instances when short-term political interests threaten those national
objectives, the head of the Federal Reserve Board, supported by the
members of the Open Market Committee, should speak up.

This is not to suggest a political battleground between central
bankers and political leaders, but the central bank should objectively
and publicly assess the impact of policies on statutory national objectives. In a not too subtle way, Mario Draghi seemed to be telling the
governments that effective monetary policy must be complemented
by appropriate fiscal measures and structural reforms. His was not
a plea to enhance the roles and powers of central banks but rather a
suggestion that politicians were avoiding tough decisions and "kick-
ing the can down the road." They were fearful of meeting the fate of
Gerhard Schroeder, who did the right thing but too late to achieve
results that might have ensured his re-election.

There is an interesting article covering a question-and-answer
session between Mohamed El-Erian, chairman of President Barack
Obama's Global Development Council, and Daniel Roth, the executive editor at LinkedIn. In his article entitled "It's Time to Take the
Economy Away From the Central Bankers," Roth comments on his
interview with El-Erian:

There are few things that keep me up at night. And until recently, I would not have included "the shaky role of central bankers" on that list. Then I read *The Only Game in Town* [*The Only Game in Town: Central Banks, Instability and Avoiding the Next Collapse*], by Allianz chief economic adviser and former Pimco CEO Mohamed El-Erian. In his book, El-Erian paints a terrifying picture of an economy that is being managed by a group of academics who never asked for the job; who don't have the tools to keep performing the task; and who have no relief in the wings. "They have been forced to make things up on the spot," El-Erian writes of the world's central bankers. "Repeatedly, they have been compelled to resort to untested policy instruments. And, with their expectations for better outcomes often disappointed, many have felt (and still feel) the need to venture ever deeper into unknown and unfamiliar policy terrains."

My take-away from the financial crisis is just the opposite. Thank goodness for central bank independence! I have never heard of a central banker claiming the right to usurp the roles of the elected representatives. But if our politicians fail to act, faced with an economic meltdown of the kind we suffered through in 2007–08, who will step in to save the ship of state from foundering? Are we to return to the system that existed in many countries where political leaders dictate monetary policy? Surely not.

As the governor of the Bank of England, Mark Carney, has said, the economy cannot be guided only by monetary policy. At the Sintra meeting, Mario Draghi seemed to be telling the political class that if they want robust open market economies they must be prepared to undertake the structural reforms and fiscal policies necessary to make them happen. Carney and Draghi were obviously right. Otherwise the economy is like a four-engine jumbo jet attempting to fly on one, which is not the way to achieve a soft landing.

ALAN GREENSPAN – A GREAT LEGACY NOTWITHSTANDING

The gathering of central bank governors and economists at the Jackson Hole Economic Policy Symposium in August 2005 was especially important in this context. It was Jackson Hole's farewell to Alan Greenspan as chairman of the Board of Governors of the Federal Reserve System. The title of the symposium that year was "The Greenspan Era: Lessons for the Future."

As was usual during that period, Thomas Hoenig, president and CEO of the Federal Reserve Bank of Kansas City, was the amiable, articulate, and gracious host. This was also my last Jackson Hole appearance because I was to step down shortly as secretary-general of the OECD. I knew I would miss this gathering of intellectual power, one of the most stimulating events I have attended.

The audience hung on every word of Greenspan's comments. He reviewed major policy changes over the decades and he graciously credited Paul Volcker, his predecessor during the Carter and Reagan years, with doing the heavy lifting in monetary policy to bring inflation under control starting in 1979. Greenspan laid great emphasis on the increasing capacity of the economy to withstand serious shocks through more resiliency and flexibility. To illustrate this point he emphasized that the 20 per cent market decline on 19 October 1987, the credit crunch of the early 1990s, and the bursting of the stock market bubble in 2000 "were absorbed with the shallowest recessions in the post WWII period." He also pointed out that even "the economic fallout from the tragic events of Sept. 11, 2001, was limited by market forces, with severe economic weakness evident for only a few weeks."

His comments were warmly received and the justifiable admiration and respect for the Greenspan era was widely shared well beyond Jackson Hole. As Tom Hoenig wrote in his introduction to the published proceedings of that meeting, "During Alan Greenspan's 18 year tenure as chairman of the Federal Reserve System, U.S. economic performance has been exceptional. Over this period, policymakers have been challenged with structural change in the form of ongoing deregulation, technological progress, and globalization."

UNBOUNDED OPTIMISM
VERSUS RAGHURAM RAJAN'S REALITY

That the bankers attending the meeting envisaged sunny skies ahead for the future of the US economy was not surprising. It was difficult to challenge the extraordinary record of Chairman Greenspan and the "resiliency and flexibility" that he credited to giving greater play to market forces in the financial services sector. Much of that, he claimed, was due to broader risk sharing through the use of derivatives. Bear in mind that this symposium was held just a few years before the beginning of the greatest recession since the 1930s.

What is particularly fascinating about the 2005 symposium, given subsequent events, was a thoughtful paper ("Financial Markets, Financial Fragility, and Central Banking") presented by Raghuram Rajan, then with the IMF. He outlined what he saw as risks inherent in the revolution of the financial services sector: "In the last 30 years, financial systems around the world have undergone revolutionary change. People can borrow greater amounts at cheaper rates than ever before, invest in a multitude of instruments catering to every possible profile of risk and return, and share risks with strangers from across the globe. Have these undoubted benefits come at a cost? How concerned should central bankers and financial system supervisors be?"

It was a brilliant analysis, but it seemed to rain on the happy parade of experts at Jackson Hole who were celebrating the successes of the Greenspan era. Rajan continued, "While it is hard to be categorical about anything as complex as the modern financial system, it is possible these developments may create more financial-sector-induced procyclicality than the past. They may also create a greater (albeit small) probability of a catastrophic meltdown."

A number of experts present, Don Kohn, Jean-Claude Trichet, Malcolm Knight, and Stanley Fischer, disagreed with the need to control or discipline these new market forces through incentives, disincentives, or regulation and, like Greenspan, believed in private regulation. As Kohn remarked, "The actions of private parties to protect themselves ... are generally quite effective."

Alan Blinder of Princeton University, a former vice chairman of the Federal Reserve System, rode to Rajan's defence with this important observation: "I'd like to defend Raghu a little bit against the unremitting attack he is getting here for not being a sufficiently good Chicago economist and just emphasize the sentence in his paper which says, 'There is typically less downside and more upside risk from generating investment returns.' This is very mildly said. The way a lot of these funds operate, you can become richer than Croesus on the upside and on the downside you just get your salary. These are extremely convex returns ... I've wondered for years why this is so."

I suspect that with the hangover from one of the worst recessions in history still lingering today, greater appreciation of Rajan's warning would have made central bankers and many economists rethink their over-reliance on "private regulation" and management incentive schemes.

Because central bankers themselves have every reason to get it right with no personal incentive except their professional reputations, I repeat my support for their critical roles, especially when politicians are constantly buffeted by the winds of political popularity fanned by pollsters and pundits.

8

Austerity versus Growth –
Ideology versus Common Sense

Earlier chapters touched upon the continuing debate between economists and their client politicians about the right approach to dealing
with the crisis flowing from the economic meltdown of 2007–08:
austerity or stimulus. To many observers, including me, the debate
often seems rooted in ideology rather than common sense. Calls for
austerity remind me of the primitive medical "cure" of bloodlet-
ting or the American soldier during the Vietnam War who allegedly
explained, "We had to destroy the village in order to save it."

BELT TIGHTENING, NOT STRANGULATION

Obviously, governments and families must reorder spending priorities to reignite adequate growth in the presence of falling income. But
the word *austerity* carries connotations of extreme sacrifice rather
than careful and focused borrowing and spending in a belt-tightening
mode. However, since *austerity* has entered the common parlance of
economists, governments, and even the general public, I will use the
word in this chapter with that caveat.

Can we have both austerity and growth? Can austerity be accompanied by increased public debt? The answer in both cases is "yes"
if faltering economies are to pull back from the looming chasm of
socio-economic collapse.

Austerity, fiscal consolidation, belt tightening, whatever one calls
it, must lay the foundations for productivity and growth without
destroying the intellectual and business infrastructure upon which

they depend. Too often governments take drastic measures to improve macroeconomic data in the near term to attract international capital at affordable interest rates. They do this without considering the collateral damage: the collapse of small- and medium-sized enterprises unable to obtain loans from a paralyzed banking sector preoccupied with trying to improve their balance sheets; massive unemployment with the risk of an outward migration of all-important human capital; and a demoralized and bitter citizenry seeing only reduced standards of living for themselves and their children for years to come.

Remember that political decision makers are very much in the hands of professional advisers when they develop and implement public policy, especially on economic matters. During an economic crisis of the kind we experienced and continue to feel the effects of, invisible economists are whispering in the ears of decision makers. As stated above, when there is no consensus among economic advisors, there is unlikely to be a consensus among political leaders. This is a problem faced by all governments.

From the diagnosis of the looming crisis, which by and large the economic community did not foresee, to the question of recovery, there is no apparent consensus among many of the best-known economists of our era. The stark division of opinions among them places a very heavy burden on political leaders who will ultimately pay the political price, or reap the political benefits, of the success or failure of the road they take.

Some economists elect to take the road called austerity, with all the negative consequences described above; others choose the road called stimulus, a more Keynesian approach to recovery. Given this dichotomy, political leaders must accept Nocera's view referenced in the previous chapter: "sometimes you just have to make up your own mind."

Can there be a sensible balance between these two roads? Can a government discipline public spending through austerity *and* stimulate growth by reallocating savings while temporarily increasing deficits without jeopardizing the political imperative of getting re-elected?

The political economy challenge is central to this approach, and there are examples from which we can draw lessons.

MOVE QUICKLY ON PAINFUL STRUCTURAL REFORMS

First, if austerity is necessary and the government enjoys the confidence of being newly elected, politicians should move quickly to introduce measures to establish sound public finances. Delaying structural reforms can sabotage re-election in democracies.

This means targeting vested interests, both social and economic. Such moves will prove unpopular in the short term, but if introduced early in an electoral mandate they may produce positive results before the competition for re-election.

The Schroeder government in Germany did this under the guidance of Agenda 2010. That agenda flowed from the recommendations of the Hartz Commission, which Schroeder had mandated near the end of his first term. The agenda contained many unpopular structural reform measures, including cuts in pension benefits and unemployment benefits, all in the name of stimulating higher economic growth with concomitant job creation.

Schroeder's economic minister, Wolfgang Clement, invited me to Berlin to speak in support of the agenda as it was compatible with the OECD recommendations for Germany's structural reforms. Clement, the finance minister, and the government made great efforts to sell Agenda 2010 to the German electorate, but the unpopularity of these essential reforms led to Schroeder's defeat, and Chancellor Angela Merkel was the beneficiary. One could say Schroeder planted the seeds and Merkel picked the fruit.

EMPHASIZE BENEFITS, NOT SACRIFICE

Second, political leaders should never suggest that such fiscal discipline and concomitant sacrifices will reduce living standards and job prospects well into the future. These negative impacts are not inevitable, and dire warnings risk encouraging the young and talented, the most important resource of the twenty-first century, to leave their native lands for opportunities elsewhere. This appeared to be happening in Spain in recent years but as recovery seems to have taken hold sooner than anticipated perhaps that trend will be reversed.

EXERCISE POLITICAL LEADERSHIP

Third, political leaders must play a central role, as President Kim Dae-jung did in South Korea during the crisis of 1997, explaining the importance of some belt tightening in the interests of economic growth, even in the short and medium term. He invited me to Korea many times during the crisis to events and to speak to reinforce his message. As a result, we developed a precious personal friendship that endured until his death in 2009.

Korea did benefit from a well-educated and resourceful population. Many citizens made personal sacrifices (like giving their jewelry and valuables to the government) to contribute to the recovery.

Koreans suffered short-term pain for long-term gain. The GDP contracted by 6.7 per cent in 1998 then expanded by 10.9 per cent in 1999. This turnaround astonished the world and economists who had prematurely predicted that the Miracle on the Han (the beautiful river that traverses Seoul on its way to the sea) had come to an end. Since that time, Korean GDP has more than doubled. Korea should serve as a positive example of strong political leadership and effective communications of the sacrifices required to secure a promising future.

Finland's recovery from its economic collapse following the disappearance of the Soviet Union took longer, but there never seemed to be a sense of despair about the future, despite the fact that there was high unemployment for most of the 1990s. GDP growth fell from 5.6 per cent in 1989 to 0 per cent in 1990 and it went deep into negative territory until the mid-1990s. Perhaps morale remained high in Finland because, unlike the Korean crisis and the more recent global one, the economic crisis had not been triggered by the greed of an elite few. The message to the Greeks and others during a severe economic downturn should be this: others have recovered rapidly from a major economic crisis, and you can too.

EMPHASIZE THE NEED FOR SACRIFICES BY ALL

So what have we learned from these boom and bust stories? Sacrifices must be made, but they must be seen as fair and must be borne by all. When private sector wages fall, everyone on the public payroll, from the prime minister on down, must also accept an income reduction. Citizens who endure individual hardship are outraged when bad governance and the self-serving greed of a privileged few combine to destroy their livelihoods and dreams of the future. Think of Occupy Wall Street.

AVOID ACROSS-THE-BOARD CUTS TO PROGRAMS

When government spending needs to be reduced, fiscal discipline should be applied with a rifle, not a shotgun. This is not an easy task, because each government department jealously protects its budget. Deadlocks are too often broken by imposing across-the-board cuts, the worst possible outcome. Sectors of the economy, and the government departments supporting them, that can spur a return to growth, job creation, and export opportunities must be protected and, if possible, strengthened. While it is clear that no one size fits all, massive public expenditure cuts in the name of austerity is not a road leading countries to growth and prosperity.

As banks write off non-performing loans and try to improve their balance sheets, public investment is critical. Governments normally have a backlog of good projects that are not immediately financeable but are "shovel ready." Funding should be allocated not just to bricks-and-mortar projects but also to investing in high-tech infrastructure in information and communication technologies, investing in public research laboratories, upgrading transportation networks, and addressing environmental challenges in agriculture, forestry, and fisheries. They must all be investments that will increase the nation's productivity and provide immediate and near-term jobs and future government tax revenues.

I know from personal experience that an appropriate balance between austerity and growth is not the impossible challenge many would have us believe. As a minister in the Canadian federal government in the early 1980s I held responsibility for an infrastructure recovery program. In the wake of "stagflation" – dismal growth, 12 per cent inflation, mounting deficits, and ballooning public debt – we injected more than $2 billion of new money into the economy, applying the criteria listed above. It worked.

Kim Dae-Jung, former president of South Korea, with his own written gift in Chinese characters (courtesy of OECD Photo OCDÉ/Silvia Thompson)

Gro Harlem Brundtland, director general of the World Health
Organization, talking with author upon her arrival at the OECD
Council (courtesy of OECD Photo OCDE/Silvia Thompson)

Minister Dominique Voynet chairing an OECD meeting of environment
ministers (courtesy of OECD Photo OCDE/Silvia Thompson)

US Secretary of State Madeleine Albright at the signing of the Anti-Bribery Convention in Paris (courtesy of OECD Photo OCDE/Silvia Thompson)

French Justice Minister Élisabeth Guigou and Finance Minister Dominique Strauss-Kahn with author at the signing of the Anti-Bribery Convention (courtesy of OECD Photo OCDE/Silvia Thompson)

US Secretary of State Colin Powell speaking with author about corruption and taxes in his office (courtesy of OECD Photo OCDE/ Silvia Thompson)

World Bank president James Wolfensohn and author signing
cooperation agreement on Corporate Governance Principles at
the OECD, Paris (courtesy of OECD Photo OCDE/Silvia Thompson)

Author with Bo Xilai, governor of Liaoning; (centre) and China Development Forum organizer Lu Mai (courtesy of Donald J. Johnston)

Vice President Al Gore thanking author for participating in the
Ethics Conference, Washington (courtesy of OECD Photo OCDE/
Silvia Thompson)

French President Jacques Chirac and author discuss genetically modified food at the Elysée Palace, Paris (courtesy of OECD Photo OCDE/Silvia Thompson)

Official visit to the OECD by Thai Prime Minister Thaksin Shinawatra
(courtesy of OECD Photo OCDE/Silvia Thompson)

9

Bubbles in our Future? Certainly!

In October 2008 Alan Greenspan called the credit crisis caused by a housing bubble a tsunami that would only occur once a century. Not long ago he could have made a similar comment about asset bubbles, which historically were decades and even a century apart.

THE DERIVATIVE FIASCO

Yet we have witnessed two bubbles within a decade: the dot-com bubble at the turn of the century and then the American housing price bubble, which had global economic consequences because of the international marketing of derivatives secured on overvalued assets, notably the subprime mortgages of American homeowners. The credit crisis Greenspan spoke about was not a direct product of an asset bubble but rather the impact on lenders who had bet on such derivatives for better rates of return during a period of very low interest yields on conservative debt instruments.

Japanese banks suffered in the same way in the 1990s after they loaned massive amounts of capital secured on highly inflated real estate values. Fortunately, those Japanese debt instruments were not engineered into derivatives and marketed around the world.

When lenders are faced with writing off massive amounts of such bad debts, their capacity to meet obligatory reserve requirements and the borrowing demands of others, such as small- and medium-sized businesses, dries up. Economic activity is stifled and jobs quickly disappear. All enterprises dependent on credit suffer, so the economy-wide knock-on effect is dramatic.

The more recent economic downturn in Spain was similar to that in Japan, with the accumulation of non-performing bank loans in the real estate sector. The capacity to lend disappeared and the lack of credit facilities carried economy-wide consequences. The tsunami to which Greenspan referred was of a different order of magnitude because it was rooted in sophisticated financial engineering that created derivative instruments secured largely on overvalued subprime mortgages of American homeowners and widely marketed both domestically and internationally.

Globalization of financial markets carries serious risks because the seamless integration of these markets enables contagion to find a convenient path across continents and the globe. Some economies, such as the Korean one, escaped much of the damage from the subprime crisis because their financial markets were not as integrated internationally as many others.

Greenspan resisted the regulation of financial derivatives and considered that they had made the banking system more resilient as evidenced in part by the fact that they remained robust despite the collapse of the dot-com bubble. In remarks to the Futures Industry Association on 19 March 1999, he commented on derivatives as follows: "The reason that growth has continued despite adversity, or perhaps because of it, is that these new financial instruments are an increasingly important vehicle for unbundling risks. These instruments enhance the ability to differentiate risk and allocate it to those investors most able and willing to take it." He believed that the burden of regulating these instruments would reduce their attractiveness.

However, in 2008, as the economic consequences of these widely held derivatives became evident, he had this to say to the House Committee on Oversight and Government Reform, as I noted in chapter 6: "Those of us who have looked to the self-interest of lending institutions to protect shareholders' equity, myself included, are in a state of shocked disbelief."

Is an unintended result of the derivative market the creation of more and more risk by those who sell such instruments knowing they will not be holding the risk themselves? Would they have had more incentive to confirm the credit worthiness and asset values of the original borrowers had at least some of that risk remained on their balance sheets? Is that not an important element of what we witnessed with the subprime crisis? Creators and sellers of such derivative instruments should continue as guarantors, jointly and severally, of the underlying value, just as endorsers of a cheque or bill of exchange do.

OTTOMAN TULIPS AND HISTORICAL PRECEDENTS

Returning to the question of bubbles, how does one foresee that there is a bubble destined to collapse? And is there some commonality between historical bubbles from which lessons can be drawn that raise red flags for investors?

Consider the tulip bubble of the seventeenth century. The Ottoman Empire supplied the first exotic tulip bulbs to the Netherlands at the end of the sixteenth century. The Dutch appetite for exotic tulips was the foundation for economic history's first infamous bubble. At the height of the bubble, we are told that an Amsterdam man was offered, but refused, 3,000 guilders – the annual income of a wealthy merchant – for a remarkable tulip bulb called Semper Augustus. To put it into perspective, shortly thereafter Rembrandt received about one half as much for painting The Night Watch, which remains a highlight of the Rijksmuseum in Amsterdam.

It was reported in the *Economist* of 4 October 2013 that in the 1630s a sailor was thrown in a Dutch jail for eating what he thought was an onion. It was in fact a tulip bulb. Apparently the value of that supposed onion equalled the cost of feeding an entire ship's crew for a year. This craze ended – the bubble burst – with the collapse of the tulip market in 1636–37.

The next major bubbles, John Law's Mississippi bubble in France and the South Sea bubble, occurred almost a century later.

BEWARE GREATER FOOLS

We have witnessed how the theory of the "greater fool" plays out in bubble creation, with each investor trapped between the emotions of greed and fear and thinking there will always be a greater fool to take his or her position. For example, the great Sir Isaac Newton was caught in the South Sea bubble. An early investor, he sensed that a crash was ahead and became fearful; he bailed out, allegedly realizing a then-handsome profit of 7,000 pounds. As he watched the stock continue to rise, greed apparently overtook Newton and he repurchased stock, ultimately losing some 20,000 pounds as the bubble collapsed. I cite the example of Newton to illustrate how irrational exuberance can take over the most rational of minds.

IDENTIFYING BUBBLES: ART OR SCIENCE?

There are strong analogies between the dot-com bubble of recent years and the South Sea bubble, and for that matter the stock market crash of 1929 where in two months the market lost 40 per cent of its value and by the end of the crash three years later was down nearly 90 per cent from its 1929 high.

Some economists say that a bubble occurs when the price of an asset, such as shares, exceeds the intrinsic underlying value of the company. Some define *intrinsic* as the value of an object, good, or service contained in the item itself. I find this an area of considerable difficulty when one talks, for example, of fundamentals such as the price-earning ratios in a particular sector as a yardstick of values. But often the shares rise far beyond that in anticipation of future earnings, which may never be realized.

Look at the situation with the dot-com phenomenon. In many cases there were no earnings at all, just irrational expectations. In some instances those anticipations may turn out to have been a great investment opportunity. Think back to the initial skepticism about the price of Google shares, which were issued in 2004 at $85 and hit $700 in late 2007.

As a contemporary example, gold prices have been very volatile since 2000, rising to about $1,900 per ounce and then falling back to less than $1,100 before achieving a modest recovery. In 2001 gold was less than $300 per ounce. Is this not a bubble in line with the tulip craze of the 1600s? What is the intrinsic value of gold today, beyond its use in commercial metal applications? At least a tulip bulb is edible, as the imprisoned Dutch sailor proved.

Many American workers and their families who had not seen meaningful income increases for many years probably relied on "bubble equity" in then-current home values to finance their children's education or purchase consumer products that they could otherwise not afford. There was certainly a strong incentive to do so.

I conclude that most bubbles are identifiable only with hindsight. Most economists failed to predict the collapse of the housing market in the United States that began in the summer of 2006. I referred in chapter 6 to Larry Summers' assertion in January of 2006 that there was no housing bubble in the United States. Because greed is a basic component of human nature I believe there will always be irrational bubbles chased by investors trying to catch them as they inflate, knowing full well that collapse may lie ahead but hoping it comes after they have made a profitable and safe retreat by benefiting from the greed of the greater fool.

10

Sustainable Development:
A Recipe with Too Many Ingredients

Manage the unmanageable whole by breaking it into manageable pieces. I should have followed this good advice when I introduced sustainable development (SD) to the OECD's work in the late 1990s. The concept of SD took life in 1987 with the Brundtland Commission's report "Our Common Future" where this definition was introduced: "Sustainable development is development that meets the needs of the present without compromising the ability of future generations to meet their own needs."

While this definition seemed good, in an international context it sowed the seeds of debate and confusion, especially within the OECD membership of advanced economies. Addressing far more than a single challenge, a biosphere in rapid ecological decline, SD was said to stand on three pillars: economic, social, and environmental.

OECD's Convention, drafted over 50 years ago, included the economic and social pillars of SD: "to achieve the highest sustainable economic growth and employment and a rising standard of living in Member countries, while maintaining financial stability, and thus to contribute to the development of the world economy." Since its inception in 1961 the OECD has pursued those two pillars. The spectacular growth of OECD economies, with accompanying improvements in public health and education and the other benefits of a prosperous democracy, are testimony to its success. From my time in the Canadian government I had a great interest in health programs for both economic and social reasons. Although I did not see health services as part of the SD work program, they certainly fell within the definition of SD in the Brundtland report.

Why did the OECD Convention not include the biosphere's natural capital as an essential element of economic growth and social development? Until Rachel Carson woke us up in 1962 with her seminal work *Silent Spring,* we took the environment for granted, assuming it would always be able to serve human needs.

In 1970 Secretary-General Emile van Lennep established the Environment Directorate and the very first intergovernmental committee dealing with the environment. Gro Harlem Brundtland, later Norway's prime minister, chaired the OECD's first Ministerial meeting on the environment in 1974. Since then all three pillars have been firmly imbedded in the organization's work program.

Gro Harlem Brundtland, a medical doctor and scientist, is rightly seen as a major force in the areas of SD and public health. She was the director general of the World Health Organization (WHO) for much of the time that I was secretary-general of the OECD. My experience in the Canadian government had convinced me that the economics of health systems was becoming a major social and financial challenge. What better place to address best practices in public health systems than the OECD? Ambassadors resisted, arguing that health was the WHO's remit and that the OECD should "stick to its knitting" of economic analysis.

With the help of my deputy secretary-general, Thorvald Moe, who had served in Harlem Brundtland's government, I persuaded her to come to Paris to tell OECD ambassadors why the OECD's economic analytical capacities were critical to support the work of the WHO, which did not have that skill set.

Convinced by her arguments and knowing her excellent reputation, the ambassadors concluded that the OECD should undertake a major project to do nationally comparative studies on the economic issues related to health and health-care systems. This experience taught me that the country representatives at the OECD are often unable to assess the value of OECD work because of their respective backgrounds.

The health project continues to this day and its analysis and recommendations are highly valued by governments struggling to deal
with increased public demand for better health care and the skyrock-
eting costs of that care largely as a result of the aging of their popu-
lations. The OECD is uniquely placed to determine why some systems
are less costly and more efficient in health-care delivery. Apart from
environmental challenges to the biosphere, human health is an obvious key to SD. I was grateful to the WHO and Gro Harlem Brundtland
for helping to get health programs on the OECD work program.

Shortly after I arrived at the OECD, Bill Long, the head of the Environment Directorate at the time, pointed out that although the organization had been a pioneer and groundbreaker on environmental
issues, a proliferation of bodies around the globe now focused on
them. Was the OECD's work really adding value?

To answer that question we established a high-level advisory group
under the co-chairmanship of Jonathan Lash of the World Resources
Institute and Stephan Schmidheiny, president of the AVINA Group in
Switzerland and sometimes described as the "Green Billionaire." In all
there were 14 members of the group, drawn from the private and public sector, all with very strong credentials: the group included Maria
Livanos Cattaui of the International Chamber of Commerce, Anna
Lindh, who was then the Swedish minister of the environment (bru-
tally assassinated in 2003), Brice Lalonde, a former French minister of
the environment, and Canadian Jim MacNeill, who had played a key
role in the Brundtland Commission in the late 1980s.

The first meeting took place over a working dinner at my Paris
residence in February 1997. Nine months later the group delivered its
final report with this powerful endorsement of the OECD's role: "Our
key recommendation is that the OECD should, as a matter of urgency,
develop into the key intergovernmental organisation providing the
industrialized nations with the analytic and comparative framework
of policy necessary for their economies to make the transition to sustainable development."

Unfortunately this strong endorsement, combined with the Brundtland definition of SD based on "needs," was about to open a Pandora's
box. The concept was subjective, ephemeral, and ever-changing: there

were an infinite number of needs, real or perceived, in every society. Looking back, I should have clearly defined the scope of the project to limit the number of issues that member countries would load into the SD basket. On the question of needs, a witness at the Brundtland Commission observed, "As people advance materially, and eat and live better, what were once luxuries tend to be regarded as necessities."

Having grown up on a small farm without indoor plumbing in an era when a one-car family was considered wealthy, I knew that luxuries are relative. It would be difficult to find common ground on needs when comparing standards of living in advanced OECD countries with those in countries at varying stages of development.

In 1997, five years after the Earth Summit in Rio, the world anxiously awaited news of progress to improve the health of the biosphere. Human survival depended upon capping and reducing greenhouse gas (GHG) emissions, especially CO_2, which scientists warned were the primary source of global warming.

The United Nations stock-taking report that year went far beyond the GHG issues and painted a dismal picture of the global environment. Here is an excerpt we received at the United Nations General Assembly in Special Session (UNGASS): "fragile ecosystems, including mountain ecosystems, are still deteriorating in all regions of the world, resulting in diminishing biological diversity. At the global level, renewable resources, in particular fresh water, forests, topsoil and marine fish stocks, continue to be used at rates beyond their viable rates of regeneration; without improved management, this situation is clearly unsustainable."

By any measure it was a very disappointing report card. Perhaps the flurry of events in 1997, UNGASS in New York and then Kyoto later that year, gave false comfort to those who believed that countries were serious about saving our natural capital and reversing the rise in CO_2 and other GHG emissions.

I fear that the exaggerated accomplishments of the December 2015 Paris Summit may repeat the Kyoto experience, again lulling the general public into thinking that if climate change is major problem, political leaders of some 195 countries are now fast-tracking to a solution. They are not. This issue is addressed in chapter 11.

Addressing this special session of the UN in New York, I emphasized the significant contribution the OECD would continue to make
to SD and the environment. That evening the US under secretary of
state for global affairs, Tim Wirth, organized a dinner at the Centro
restaurant for a high-level group to discuss the way forward and
OECD's role. The dinner included Maurice Strong, who had organized
the UN Stockholm Conference of 1972 and later the Rio Earth Summit of 2002.

It was clear that the evolution of the world after Rio had failed to
meet the minimal hopes and expectations of dedicated people like
Wirth and the others gathered around the table. The following year
Tim left government to head Ted Turner's $1 billion UN foundation
on the environment. He has since left that post for other personal
priorities.

That dinner provided me with the opportunity to meet the new
UK deputy prime minister, John Prescott, who also held responsibility for the environment, transport, and regions. This combination
of portfolios was intriguing. It would give the environment ministry
heavyweight cabinet clout, which was not common in most countries
at that time. I wondered whether the absence of senior ministers with
responsibility for the environment had contributed to this marked
lack of progress, a shared concern around the table that evening.

Prescott was outspoken. He came across as a straight shooter, a
touch pugnacious perhaps (as evidenced by much TV coverage of
him punching a farmer who threw an egg at him during a campaign
stop), no doubt a product of his front-line trade union battles. I
would have a number of other interesting encounters with this New
Labour Blairite in subsequent years.

I left the dinner encouraged by its focus on the environmental pillar of SD but feeling a heavy load of responsibility. It was clear that
the OECD, with its economic analytical capability and interdisciplinary approaches, should be a critical player in the pursuit of global
SD. No other organization could bring the same intellectual artillery
to bear on the subject or benefit from the direct pipeline to decision
makers that we had through our committee system.

But would OECD governments acknowledge that the environment

was the cornerstone of SD? Would they support recommendations to reduce subsidies to fossil fuel development and its use as the primary energy source? Would they ask the OECD to use its rich analytical skills to create fair carbon taxes or effective cap and trade regimes?

Unfortunately, many countries remained wed to the Brundt-land Commission's definition of SD. I found this aggravating. I had launched the OECD's SD work to address the pressing issues of bio-sphere protection and to examine the possible social implications of economic instruments designed to do that. Taxing water consump-tion was an obvious example. Many saw it as a sensible approach to fresh water management and conservation, but what were the eco-nomic and social consequences for agriculture and the poor?

Each member country had its own priorities. So many issues were being heaped into SD's three pillars that the work was billowing out of control. Even a review of Slovakia's pension system was classified as part of the SD mandate. It was a good illustration of the marriage of the three pillars in wealthy countries, but sustainable pensions are hardly of interest to the billions in developing countries who have no salaries, let alone pensions.

Although 1997 was a landmark year for SD with the report of the high-level advisory group at the OECD, the UNGASS, the announce-ment of Ted Turner's billion-dollar foundation, and the adoption of the Kyoto Protocol, the question remained: What concrete policies that were suitable for international implementation would emerge? There was lots of vacuous political rhetoric, to be sure, but what else was there of value to save the biosphere? Would another five or ten years pass without coordinated international action to make the environmental pillar of global SD a priority? Of course, twenty years later we know the sad answer to that question.

The Kyoto Protocol raised public expectations to unreasonable heights. Most people thought that its universal adoption and appli-cation could lay to rest concerns about climate change and global warming. The science told us otherwise. The protocol was a step in the right direction but could only retard global warming by a few years. And with the United States, the world's greatest emitter of GHGs, not a signatory, even that small step was beyond reach. China, today the largest global emitter of GHGs, escaped much of the discipline of the protocol as a developing nation.

ROUND TABLE ON SUSTAINABLE DEVELOPMENT

To speed progress on the issues of global concern, in 1998 I created the Round Table on Sustainable Development, which was attached to the OECD but financed by outside contributions. External funding would, I hoped, avoid the necessity of including all countries around the table and the inevitable political posturing found in other fora.

Once again I enlisted Thorvald Moe's assistance. Like his former prime minister, Gro Harlem Brundtland, he had a deep interest in environmental issues and brought his experience as a former OECD ambassador and economist to this initiative.

Simon Upton, the dynamic young New Zealand minister of the environment and chair of the UN Commission on Sustainable Development, accepted my invitation to chair the round table, which he was able to do on a full-time basis after he left politics in 2001. He put the round table at the forefront of SD international discussions and debates. The OECD website accurately describes the round table as follows:

> The Round Table on Sustainable Development was established in 1998 to provide an informal setting through which ministers can engage one another and key international business and civil society leaders without prejudice to negotiating positions on cross-cutting issues.
>
> In May 2001, OECD Ministers formally endorsed the role of the Round Table "as a forum for international dialogue among stakeholders." The following year, OECD Ministers again singled out the Round Table and requested that it continue to "generate policy ideas and build consensus for action" to assist them in achieving their "sustainable development objectives."
>
> No other ministerial-level forum gathers such a diverse group. Preparation of the subject matter is intensive and includes an independent paper written specifically for each

meeting. By keeping participation limited and exclusive to the topic, following the Chatham House rule and not allowing bureaucrats to substitute for politicians, the Round Table provides a rare opportunity for high-level attendees to engage on a direct and in-depth basis. As a result, they are free to test out their thinking and spontaneously promote future action.

Specifically, the Round Table only places on its agenda issues that:

- are truly global in scope and require the collective engagement of global level players if they are to be moved forward;
- are cross-cutting in the sense that their resolution requires engagement by several policy communities and/or decision-making groups;
- prove to be extremely difficult to advance through more formal and familiar channels and showing little prospect of immediate progress.

In a short time more than a hundred ministers attended, meeting with senior members of the international business community, academics, and representatives of international organizations including the UN and the World Bank. One of the World Bank's vice presidents, Ian Johnson, played a very active and supportive role.

The round table continued after my departure from the OECD with Simon Upton, who later became the head of the Environment Directorate, as its chair. He has now been replaced in that role by Connie Hedegaard, a Danish politician who also spent four years as the European commissioner for climate action.

MORE MANDATE OVERREACH

In May 2001 the OECD's three-year work program on SD culminated in a meeting of environment ministers back to back with the annual Ministerial Council Meeting of economy, finance, and trade ministers and the OECD Forum of representatives from civil society, academia, business, and unions. Energy ministers from member countries of the International Energy Agency, which is linked to the OECD, were meeting at the same time, completing the team of all the major players critical to advancing the SD agenda.

I convinced esteemed Harvard biologist E.O. Wilson, author of the 1998 bestselling book *Consilience: The Unity of Knowledge*, to address the OECD Forum in 2001. He struck an important nerve in all present when he said:

> Exploitation of the natural environment is growing at an unsustainable rate, ultimately risking human survival itself. Economists have long ignored the real cost of environmental degradation, because they do not use the right statistics. The key statistic for measuring sustainability is called the ecological footprint – the average amount of productive land and coastal marine environment appropriated by each person around the world for survival. In the developing world, which has 5 billion of the earth's 6 billion population, that footprint is about 2.5 acres per person. That compares with a footprint of around 24 acres in the United States. For every person in the world to reach US levels of consumption with existing technology would require four more planet earths.

Wilson has a way of dramatizing the environmental challenges we face. For example, in a celebrated quotation he is recorded as saying, "Destroying rainforest for economic gain is like burning a Renaissance painting to cook a meal."

Dominique Voynet, France's colourful minister of the environment, chaired the environment Ministerial. A Green activist for many years, she was a lively interlocutor (which seemed at odds with her professional training as an anesthetist). A firm believer in broad consultation with NGOs, she invited them to participate in the opening minutes of the Ministerial session. Ministers around the table accepted this without complaint; in past meetings stakeholders had been invited to make opening statements to ministers and then leave as confidential Ministerial discussions got underway.

Then, to the astonishment of all present, including me, she invited them to sit as observers throughout the Ministerial proceedings. Surveying the room, I detected body language of considerable discomfiture by many ministers present. But who would dare speak out against Voynet's proposal in front of this array of powerful international NGOs? She knew that. Sitting next to her, I think I detected a quiet giggle of satisfaction at this coup. The British ambassador of the day, Christopher Crabbie, took me aside for a verbal assault about this episode as if I had stage-managed this unprecedented degree of ministerial transparency.

The annual Ministerial Council Meeting followed with the joint participation of economic, finance, and environment ministers. The Danish minister was chairing that Ministerial, and as I looked to the end of the table where Dominique Voynet and Laurent Fabius, then Lionel Jospin's minister of the economy, were sitting together, it seemed a very good but rare collaboration of interests.

The ministers' final communiqué ("Ministerial Communiqué: Towards a Sustainable Future," May 2001) mandated the OECD to assist member countries' efforts to formulate and implement policies to achieve SD by:

- developing agreed indicators that measure progress across all three dimensions of sustainable development, including decoupling of economic growth from environmental degradation, with a view to incorporating these into oecd's economic, social and environmental peer review processes, and filling gaps in the statistical and scientific data;
- identifying how obstacles to policy reforms, in particular to the better use of market-based instruments, and to the reduction of environmentally harmful subsidies, can be overcome; and deepening its analytical work on these instruments;
- analysing further the social aspects of sustainable development, including work on human and social capital, as well as their interaction with their economic and environmental dimensions;

• providing guidance for achieving improved economic, environmental and social policy coherence and integration.

Once again I felt we were the victims of overreach, with a grab bag of issues both domestic and global that was too vast to be meaningful.

We were now on the eve of the 2002 Johannesburg World Summit on Sustainable Development where the OECD would be presenting its work.

THE UNITED STATES IN DENIAL

On the real issues of global sustainability – energy, global warming, and climate change – the Bush administration was still largely in denial. Given America's place in the global economy, this was bound to stymie real progress. The US delegation at the OECD did not want the term *climate change* to be used in our documents, fearing that it would look as though they agreed with the view of scientists around the globe that human activity was the root cause of GHG emissions and hence global warming and climate change.

I had great sympathy for Christine Todd Whitman, who had left the governorship of New Jersey to become the administrator of the US Environmental Protection Agency. She must have assumed that she could influence the Bush administration. It was not to be. When I visited her splendiferous Washington offices in the old premises of the Postmaster General, she was far from the cheerful soul I had met on past occasions at Davos. I suspect she will always regret accepting the post, thereby joining the ranks of Paul O'Neill at the Treasury and Colin Powell at State.

Given her outstanding environmental record as governor of New Jersey, I wondered how much her efforts were stalled or undermined by the White House. Sadly, she left the Environmental Protection Agency in 2003 with a largely unfinished agenda. Her book *It's My Party Too: The Battle for the Heart of the GOP and the Future of America* makes it apparent that she was uncomfortable in the administration and appalled at the Republican Party's hijacking of environmental protection by what she called the social fundamentalists.

The World Summit on Sustainable Development happened on her watch and she dutifully went to Johannesburg to defend the indefensible positions of the United States, much as Colin Powell defended the invasion of Iraq before the UN Security Council on the false pretense that Saddam Hussein had weapons of mass destruction.

The summit in Johannesburg attracted thousands, including much of the world's leadership. That was the good news. It was also positive that Kofi Annan focused largely on environmental and development issues and not on the panoply of sustainable "needs" of developed countries.

The bad news was more sobering. Ten years after the Earth Summit in Rio, it was painfully clear that efforts had fallen far short of the goals.

What has to be done to slow, stop, and reduce GHG emissions is well known. But the work of the UN's Intergovernmental Panel on Climate Change (IPCC) and a host of other organizations including responsible NGOs has failed to muster the political will to move forward aggressively within major economies. The Paris outcome could be different, but this is very unlikely, especially since its targets are too modest and carry no sanctions.

The summit in Johannesburg took place fifteen years after the publication of the Brundtland Commission's "Our Common Future," ten years after the Rio Earth Summit, and thirty years after the UN Stockholm meeting. The UN had mandated the Brundtland Commission to propose long-term strategies to attain global SD by the year 2000, but we found ourselves in 2002 with the same challenges and problems that the commission had identified fifteen years earlier.

Now, nearly 30 years after that groundbreaking report was released, we are still faced with rising poverty, biodiversity loss, increases in the generation of solid waste, increasing GHG emissions, groundwater pollution, diminishing marine resources, shortages of fresh water in many areas, and the prospect of climate change's apocalyptic consequences. We were and are treading on a number of unsustainable paths at the same time.

SEPARATING NATIONAL AND GLOBAL
ISSUES OF SUSTAINABLE DEVELOPMENT

As we attempt to meet the challenge of SD we must separate local and national from global issues. Only the environment, the biosphere's natural capital, enjoys a common planetary constituency. So when we speak about SD we must decide whether we are addressing issues of global sustainability or national interests. National interests will vary depending upon each country's level of social and economic development. In countries where people are well educated, housed, and fed, concerns about the next generation will be quite different from those in countries where development means lower rates of poverty, disease, malnutrition, and infant mortality.

If we accept the concept of the global village as it is described in the Brundtland Report, we must address the issue of sustainability for the village as a whole, not just for a few affluent communities. We must build the sustainability of the planet on a green environmental foundation: the air we all breathe, the water, the soil we cultivate, and biodiversity.

Remedial action to reverse the overall degradation of the biosphere will require many complementary strategies, which include alleviating poverty in the developing world. Can we wean ourselves off fossil fuels and in the interim reduce CO_2 and other emissions before we cross a threshold of atmospheric concentrations that could trigger radical and abrupt climate change? I am doubtful that we can do this, and I explain why in the following chapter. We may be forced to consider radical solutions such as geoengineering to prevent intolerable global temperature increases.

Climate Change: Unrealistic Expectations

In the previous chapter I described the vast challenges of sustainable development (SD). A healthy environment is the foundation of all SD. It is being threatened by increased global warming through GHG emissions, notably CO_2. The marked increases in emissions arise from anthropogenic sources, namely human activities.

The IPCC has been publishing interdisciplinary reports on global warming and climate change since 1988. It is clear from the IPCC's consistent and comprehensive work that global warming and climate change will very probably be the most important global issue for many decades to come, if not for the next 100 years. In short, the global warming and climate change crisis speaks to the very continuation of our civilization.

RIO 1992 TO PARIS 2015

Many have argued that it is still not too late to embark upon ambitious environmental programs to ensure that GHGs decline before CO_2 accumulations in the atmosphere exceed 450 parts per million (ppm). This is the level, sometimes called the tipping point, above which global mean surface temperatures are likely to exceed pre-industrial levels by 2°C according to the scientific consensus of the IPCC, resulting in disastrous climate change consequences.

Some 195 country delegations, mostly led by presidents or prime ministers, gathered at the 21st Conference of the Parties (COP21) in Paris in early December 2015 in what many described as a last-ditch attempt to produce an international agreement to meet the two-degree challenge. I observed the conference and participated in some related side events. I sent back the following brief comment, which was published in the *Montreal Gazette* (18 December 2015):

As matters settle down in Paris after the marathon debates at the climate summit, assessments of the outcome are being offered from many quarters: academics, scientists, NGOs and politicians in particular.

Having written a piece in this space just a few weeks ago ("There is no Planet B" Opinion, Nov. 14) expressing pessimism about the probable outcome of the summit, I wish to add my own perspectives.

In my earlier commentary I tried to dampen expectations of many who saw this as a last-ditch attempt to save the planet. I did so by placing the United Nations Framework Convention on Climate Change process in historical perspective. I held no illusions about how successful countries would be in establishing binding commitments to achieve their "intended national determined contributions."

I do not see the summit as a failure. While I remain convinced that the 2-degree C challenge remains well beyond reach, several good things emerged that made the exercise worthwhile.

First, there was recognition across almost 200 countries from every part of the planet that global warming is here, is already wreaking huge cost in human and financial terms on all continents, and that human activity is responsible.

Second, there was an admission that despite the submission of national targets to reduce greenhouse-gas emissions, especially the villain CO_2, they collectively are not enough to keep the rise in global mean surface temperatures below 2 degrees C (compared with the pre-industrial period), the trigger point for the catastrophic scenarios described by the Intergovernmental Panel on Climate Change.

Third, it is clear that the process of seeking further reductions must continue under rigorous peer group pressure to keep hopes

alive of any success in meeting the 2-degree challenge in time
to avert the worst climate-change scenarios.

Fourth, there was agreement to fund poor countries, many of
which are most vulnerable, to protect themselves through adaptation to the dire consequences of climate change.

Fifth, Canada made a positive impression. Having long been
part of the problem, Canada is now seen as part of the solution.

Another reason to be pleased with the outcome is that
undoubtedly more mitigation – steps to limit the magnitude and
slow the rate of GHG emissions – will be undertaken.

However, Paris also left in its wake profound disappointment
and concern ... There remains a failure to address the most likely
future with concrete measures, namely one of much higher global
temperatures.

The atmospheric concentrations of CO_2 will probably pass
450 ppm and if the scientific consensus is right, global mean
surface temperatures will be greater than 2 degrees C. Even in the
unlikely event that all the national targets submitted to the Paris
COP21 meeting are met, that threshold would be substantially
exceeded with temperatures rising accordingly.

Where is Plan B? There is none. We are simply re-embarking
on the well-trodden path of consistent failure.

In a commentary in the *New York Times* [13 December 2015],
noted environmentalist Bill McKibben states: "In the hot, sod-
den mess that is our planet as 2015 drags to a close, the pact
reached in Paris feels, in a lot of ways, like an ambitious agreement designed for about 1995, when the first conference of the
parties to the United Nations Framework Convention on Climate
change took place in Berlin."

I agree with that comment, but I remain more optimistic about
the consequences of failure to find the silver bullet at Paris.

For example, we see ... Bill Gates's efforts to marshal billionaire support in the search for new technological innovations;
hopefully, there will be more efforts to address the challenges of
adaptation, not just in the developing world, but planet wide.
Perhaps as a last resort, atmospheric geoengineering will be

considered, at least at an experimental level to determine whether we might have a useful fire extinguisher at hand when there is a consensus that rising above 2 degrees C is inevitable.

The *Independent* newspaper (13 December 2015) reported that distinguished scientist James Hansen was less charitable about COP21:

> A leading climate scientist has denounced the Paris climate change agreement as a "fraud" – saying there is "no action, just promises." Professor James Hansen – credited as being the "father of climate change awareness" – told the *Guardian* the talks that culminated in a deal on Saturday were just "worthless words." Speaking as the final draft of the deal was published on Saturday afternoon, he said: "It's just b******t for them to say: 'We'll have a 2C warming target and then try to do a little better every five years.' It's just worthless words. There is no action, just promises. As long as fossil fuels appear to be the cheapest fuels out there, they will be continued to be burned."

Hansen has never been an irrational alarmist, and his record of climate change predictions to date has been remarkably good.

With no sanctions and no carbon pricing agreed upon in Paris, is it realistic to assume that the world, with total primary energy consumption more than 85 per cent dependent on fossil fuels in 2015, will restructure our societies and infrastructures in time to prevent CO_2 atmospheric concentrations from passing the possible tipping point? At the time of the Kyoto Protocol in 1997, concentrations were about 367 ppm. They have now passed 400 ppm and continue to rise. The US Energy Information Administration's "International Energy Outlook 2016" (May 2016) states the following: "Even though consumption of nonfossil fuels is expected to grow faster than consumption of fossil fuels, fossil fuels still account for 78% of energy use in 2040."

When we look at the experience over the last few decades of a few brave countries that have tried to come to grips with global warming and climate change, we see that the challenge is that none of our alternative solution technologies, as presently configured, is capable of being scaled up to make a significant dent in the overwhelming use of inexpensive and very convenient fossil fuels (gas, oil, and coal). Consider, for example, the situation in Germany: that country increased its wind- and solar-generated renewable electricity generating capacity (MW) to an extraordinary 44 per cent of total electricity generating capacity by the end of 2015, but these renewable sources only account for about 8 per cent of Germany's total primary energy consumption. As strongly emphasized by the US Energy Information Administration in its May 2016 report, the massive population growth in developing countries and their fast-rising standards of living and expectations are forecast to sustain the use of fossil fuels globally at very high levels for decades.

As these projections were made after the Paris COP21 targets were set, how can one not be a skeptic about the likelihood of keeping CO_2 accumulations below 450 ppm? In the absence of herculean, unprecedented efforts in research and development to find breakthrough solutions and alternatives and extraordinary global cooperation and coordination, it is too late.

The process under the United Nations Framework Convention on Climate Change has delivered agreements, but only minimal results. COP21 in Paris has maintained that dismal record of underachievement.

Despite the cynicism of Hansen and many other experts, we should applaud the fact that the world's leaders at least now acknowledge that climate change, with concomitant global warming, is real and that increasing GHG emissions (especially CO_2) are generated primarily from the use of fossil fuels. What is discouraging is that science has known of the characteristics of CO_2 and its greenhouse effect on our planet for more than a century. What have we done about it?

As early as 1896, a Swedish scientist, Svante Arrhenius (Nobel Prize for Chemistry, 1903) identified the warming effects of the CO_2 emitted by burning coal. Alarm bells rang at the Stockholm UN environmental conference in 1972 – more than 40 years ago. Concern was expressed about emissions, but their measurement and impact were not broadly understood until the UN creation of the IPCC in 1988. The alarm bells rang louder after the UN's Brundtland report ("Our Common Future") was released in 1987, and especially after the UN's Earth Summit in Rio in 1992, where the climate change convention was adopted.

The UN General Assembly in Special Session met in New York in 1997, where we listened to statements from world leaders and others (including me) about the importance of reducing emissions. That meeting was followed by the UN Kyoto conference, at which the Kyoto Protocol was adopted. It was agreed that Annex 1 countries (37 developed countries) would reduce their emissions during two commitment periods by an average of 5.2 per cent below their respective 1990 levels. Canada's commitment was a 6 per cent decrease from 1990 levels by 2012. By 2008 Canada's emissions had increased by 24.1 per cent over 1990 levels, and Canada withdrew from the protocol.

DOES POLITICAL SHORT-TERMISM DOOM THE PLANET?

We have witnessed governments across the globe tailor their policies to meet short-term political imperatives rather than long-term challenges such as climate change. Here is a stunning example from a report from the 18 July 2015 edition of *New Scientist*, just months before France hosted the COP21 climate change summit: "French President François Hollande did not turn up as scheduled to deliver the opening address at a major climate science conference in Paris last week. No doubt the Grexit crisis demanded his attention. Instead, while scientists from around the world flew in and out to discuss the future under various climate change scenarios, it emerged during the week that Hollande's government plans to quietly renege on a climate promise France made last year. It will now continue to subsidize the building of coal-fired power stations in other countries, to save jobs at the French companies that construct them."

Has the Paris summit changed this political short-termism? The great American historian, sociologist, and critic Lewis Mumford once opined: "I'm a pessimist about probabilities; I'm an optimist about possibilities." That is where I was over a decade ago. Today, I am also pessimistic about the possibilities.

What might have been possible even a decade ago has disappeared through failure to act. Decades ago, it might have been possible to embrace nuclear energy globally, particularly the critically needed research and development for a new breed of generation IV nuclear plants that could be "walk-away" safe and use more than 90 per cent of the nuclear fuel fed to the plant (not less than 5 per cent as used in our present plants). We did not.

Decades ago, there was the prospect of carrying out the critically needed research and development to develop breakthrough technologies for implementing carbon capture and sequestration. We did not.

Decades ago, there was also the prospect of carrying out the critically needed research and development to develop real breakthrough technologies for efficient, cost-effective, environmentally friendly methods for storing and using intermittent, non-reliable renewable energy (e.g., wind and solar electricity). We did not.

For many years, we have witnessed a parade of alternative energy advocates producing "possible" ways to reduce GHG emissions: wind energy, solar energy, energy efficiency, tidal energy, geothermal energy, and others make up that list. They are all great ideas, but they ignore the technical, political, and economic challenges involved in effectively integrating them and weaning ourselves and our economies off fossil fuels while meeting the world's energy requirements, in the short time remaining to us for action. To say those challenges are daunting would be an understatement. In 2015, worldwide wind and solar energy consumption amounted to less than 3 per cent of global primary energy consumption.

Think of this. Many were pleased by US President Barack Obama's declaration that the United States would cut 32 per cent of CO_2 emissions from power plants by 2030. This was good news, but as *New Scientist* pointed out in its 8 August 2015 edition, "while the plan could bring big cuts in power plant emissions, it will only cut US emissions by 6 per cent overall. A cut of 80 per cent is required to prevent dangerous global warming."

The outcome of the Paris summit will not keep us under the 450 ppm level for CO_2 accumulations and intolerable increased warming, never mind the 350 ppm level suggested by prominent US climate expert James Hansen. The planet is destined to suffer more drought, loss of agricultural land, famine, torrential rainfalls and massive flooding, ice storms, unbearable heat waves and forest fires, acidification of the seas and loss of marine life, rising sea levels perhaps of several metres as glaciers melt (and the Greenland ice cap even slides into the seas as some suggest it might), and the spread of tropical diseases to northern countries, as well as the migration of millions of people from uninhabitable regions.

To be more specific, in 2014, former New York mayor Michael Bloomberg co-chaired a non-partisan commission on climate change impacts that could affect the United States. While the commission's conclusions were US focused, they apply to varying degrees across the planet. Here is an excerpt from a Reuters' comment (24 June 2012) on the report:

> Called "Risky Business," the report projects climate impacts at scales as small as individual counties. Its conclusions about crop losses and other consequences are based not on computer projections, which climate-change skeptics routinely attack, but on data from past heat waves.
>
> It paints a grim picture of economic loss. "Our economy is vulnerable to an overwhelming number of risks from climate change," [commission co-chair Henry] Paulson said in a statement, including from sea-level rise and from heat waves that will cause deaths, reduce labor productivity and strain power grids.
>
> By mid-century, $66 billion to $106 billion worth of coastal property will likely be below sea level. There is a 5 percent chance that by 2100 the losses will reach $700 billion, with average annual losses from rising oceans of $42 billion to $108 billion along the Eastern Seaboard and Gulf of Mexico.
>
> Extreme heat, especially in the Southwest, Southeast and upper Midwest, will slash labor productivity as people are unable to work outdoors at construction and other jobs for sustained

periods. The analysis goes further than previous work, said Princeton's [Michael] Oppenheimer, by identifying places that will be "unsuited for outdoor activity."

Demand for electricity will surge as people need air conditioning just to survive, straining generation and transmission capacity. That will likely require the construction of up to 95 gigawatts of generation capacity over the next 5 to 25 years, or roughly 200 average-size coal or natural gas power plants.

If we do not reduce GHG emissions and reduce CO_2 accumulations in the atmosphere, every country will be affected in similar ways, and as the commission's report points out, massive expenditures on adaptation will be required, often in poor countries.

CO_2 is the main villain in creating the greenhouse effect because it remains in the atmosphere for up to 100 years. The volume of CO_2 in the atmosphere has continued to increase since the Industrial Revolution. It does not prevent the sun's rays from reaching and heating the earth but it traps more and more of the infrared or radiant heat emitted by the earth under this greenhouse blanket. Much of that radiant heat would otherwise be reflected back into space. Methane, which has a shorter atmospheric lifespan, can also play a significant role because it is a more potent GHG; in a twenty-year horizon, the IPCC's 2013 report shows that one kilogram of methane has eighty-six times the global warming "punching" power of one kilogram of CO_2.

Professor Granger Morgan at Carnegie Mellon University has likened the phenomenon of CO_2 atmospheric accumulation to a bathtub with a large inflowing faucet but a small drain. The CO_2 comes in, stays, and only gradually is absorbed into the seas, forests, and vegetation over many years. It will still accumulate unless the absorption rate exceeds the volume of emissions.

Of course much of the warmth generated by the sun's rays was always trapped in our atmosphere, keeping the earth at a temperature enabling life to develop. This is about 13.88°C. We have lived in a so-called Goldilocks environment that we are now searching for elsewhere in the universe. But with the incredible increase in CO_2 emissions since the beginning of the Industrial Revolution, in roughly 1760, much more of the warmth generated by the sun's rays is trapped because of the greenhouse effect.

In summary, the present policy paralysis illustrates our incapacity to come to grips with global warming and its impact on climate change, providing the weather aberrations that we witness on a daily basis.

As Secretary-General Michel Jarraud of the World Meteorological Organization reported to the UN meeting on climate change in Lima at COP20:

> The provisional information for 2014 means that fourteen of the fifteen warmest years on record have all occurred in the twenty-first century. There is no standstill in global warming. What we saw in 2014 is consistent with what we expect from a changing climate. Record-breaking heat combined with torrential rainfall and floods destroyed livelihoods and ruined lives. What is particularly unusual and alarming this year are the high temperatures of vast areas of the ocean surface, including in the northern hemisphere. Record-high greenhouse gas emissions and associated atmospheric concentrations are committing the planet to a much more uncertain and inhospitable future.

The planet faces enormous challenges if we do not want that "uncertain and inhospitable future" as well as the enormous costs foreseen by the Bloomberg commission. At the Paris COP21 meeting in December 2015, developed nations considered making a very small contribution, on a non-binding basis, to help the developing countries cope with global warming and climate change. The November 2016 COP22 meeting in Marrakech restated the commitment: "We, the Developed Country Parties, reaffirm our USD$100 billion mobilization goal."

It is likely that many times that amount must be spent annually on adaptation and critical research and development globally if we are to find the desperately needed breakthrough technological solutions to wean our civilization off of fossil fuels. Is spending of that magnitude likely? This is a rhetorical question of the first order. We have yet to see any consensus on a Plan B.

NEW THINKING, NEW TECHNOLOGIES, ATMOSPHERIC GEOENGINEERING?

I hope that as the realization takes hold that the 450 ppm threshold will be passed, international consensus will emerge and adaptation measures will be brought forward to address some of the most damaging early consequences of global warming described by the Bloomberg commission. If nuclear energy continues to be rejected as a global solution, then in the absence of some yet-to-be-discovered breakthrough technological developments, surely a Plan B must also examine solar radiation management (SRM) and broader use of carbon capture and sequestration.

There are now calls from serious sources to at least engage in testing SRM to determine whether it could serve as a lifeboat of last resort should the efforts to arrest and reduce CO_2 emissions continue to fail as they have for decades; some experts, such as David Keith at Harvard, Granger Morgan at Carnegie Mellon, and Ken Caldeira have started this work. Serious environmentalists like Bill Gates and Richard Branson are apparently interested in geoengineering.

Here is a non-technical explanation of SRM. By spreading aerosols with reflective particles in the atmosphere one could alter the albedo (i.e., the reflective capacity of the earth). This would lessen the amount of radiation that penetrates to the earth's surface, and thereby lessen the radiant heat that is trapped under the CO_2 blanket. The measured reduction in the earth's temperature resulting from the spread of volcanic ash after eruptions suggests that this would be an effective and relatively inexpensive approach. It would not be a permanent answer, and it would have to be renewed periodically. David Keith explains the concept well in his recent book entitled *A Case for Climate Engineering* (MIT Press, 2013).

Unfortunately, there is considerable resistance to the concept from two camps. The first is comprised of the dedicated environmentalists, who believe that exploring this technology may detract from the mitigation efforts of those seeking to arrest and reduce GHG emissions, especially CO_2. In the second camp are people who are fearful of even limited testing, which they claim could result in unintended consequences, and who remain convinced that there will be technological breakthroughs that will make geoengineering of the atmosphere unnecessary. The first camp remains optimistic that mitigation will be successful at five minutes to midnight even though it has failed for decades, and the second one implicitly recognizes that mitigation will fall short of its objectives but remains hopeful that there is some technology likely to emerge in time to save the planet from the consequences of severe global warming.

Surely it is irresponsible for this generation not to have a Plan B should both of these optimistic viewpoints prove incorrect. Keith thinks so. Here is an extract of the publisher's blurb for *A Case for Climate Engineering*:

> A leading scientist long concerned about climate change, Keith offers no naïve proposal for an easy fix to what is perhaps the most challenging question of our time; climate engineering is no silver bullet. But he argues that after decades during which very little progress has been made in reducing carbon emissions we must put this technology on the table and consider it responsibly. That doesn't mean we will deploy it, and it doesn't mean that we can abandon efforts to reduce greenhouse gas emissions. But we must understand fully what research needs to be done and how the technology might be designed and used.

Note this comment from Bill Gates on the book cover: "The negative effects of climate change will disproportionately impact the world's poor. David Keith's candid and thoughtful book lays out a compelling argument about the need for serious research on geo engineering and for a robust policy discussion on its possible use."

Fortunately, interest seems to be increasing in this area, which might provide breathing room for mitigation to become more successful or for new technologies to be discovered. Of course, as discussed below, nuclear energy remains the most promising source of global energy production. The new generation of nuclear plants may satisfy the objections to the existing "fleet" of nuclear plants, including their past safety record, the very low percentage use of the nuclear fuel placed in the plants, the resulting significant percentage of "spent" nuclear fuel, and the very long and highly radioactive life of the spent nuclear fuel associated with the plants, which have effectively delayed the realization of nuclear energy's potential.

WHERE IS THE NUCLEAR POWER WE NEED?

Why are we hoping for some wonderful technological breakthrough when we already have one? Nuclear power can be abundant; it produces no GHGs of any consequence. The problem is that we have put nuclear power generation on hold for too many years. As stated above, even a massive global commitment to nuclear energy at this stage would not be in time to sufficiently arrest the CO_2 we are pumping into the atmosphere and then decrease CO_2 accumulations.

The US Department of Energy said in its *International Energy Outlook 2016* report (11 May 2016) that "by 2040, almost two-thirds of the world's primary energy will be consumed in the non-OECD economies ... Even though consumption of nonfossil fuels is expected to grow faster than consumption of fossil fuels, fossil fuels still account for 78% of energy use in 2040."

Having examined the best evidence available to me, I have concluded that if we are to hand on to future generations a planet that will meet their needs as we have met ours, it can only be done by incorporating the nuclear energy option. The goal would be to slow climate change to facilitate adaptation and to further develop the potential of renewable energy, probably wind and solar.

Think of this paradox. In my youth, despite the horrors of Hiroshima and Nagasaki or the end of the Second World War, President Eisenhower's initiative of "atoms for peace" was broadly embraced as the way of the future. William Laurence wrote in the *New York Times* on 15 August 1955 that scientists at a major international conference in Geneva had indicated that thanks to nuclear energy, "for the first time, man is assured of a virtually unlimited supply of energy."

At that time, nuclear energy was seen as a godsend for both the developed and the developing world. Fossil fuels were understood to have a finite life, which of course they still do, although their life has been modestly extended beyond the estimates of that day. But fossil fuels were not seen at the time as harbouring the potential for irreversible damage to the biosphere, which we now know to be the case.

Today, the atmosphere is being choked by GHG emissions, global temperatures are rising dramatically, and the global population has more than doubled since 1955 to about 7.4 billion today. The world's population is forecast to reach 9.7 billion in 2050 and 11.2 billion by 2100, with most people probably living in poverty in the developing world. Yet we seem to be denying ourselves the nuclear option, which was seen over four decades ago as the way forward.

What happened to change public, and hence political, attitudes toward nuclear energy? It seems to be obvious that the incidents at Three Mile Island, Chernobyl, and Fukushima have had a major negative impact on the evolution of the nuclear industry. The current nuclear plants are not "walk-away" safe nor do they meet the other safety promises of the new generation IV breed of nuclear plants that are presently on the drawing board. It is likely that the tendency of the nuclear industry to secrecy, probably inherited from the national defence orientations of nuclear research, has made things worse. There are also legitimate concerns about nuclear waste disposal and operational safety and fears about the proliferation of nuclear weapons. The latter have been strengthened by the advent of ISIS and global terrorism.

I am convinced that there are good solutions to these challenges. In any event, we already have them, largely with older nuclear generators. Specifically, according to the Nuclear Energy Institute, as of May 2016 there are 444 nuclear reactors in operation across the planet; there are sixty-three reactors under construction in fifteen countries; and thirteen countries depend upon nuclear energy for at least 25 per cent of their electricity, with France depending on it for 76.3 per cent of its electricity. Had the world followed the French example we would not be faced with the challenge of global climate change today.

In 2015, nuclear energy represented less than 5 per cent of total global primary energy consumption. But the concerns about waste disposal, operational safety, and proliferation exist whether there are 500 or several thousand nuclear reactors in operation.

Because a nuclear incident has implications far beyond the border of the country where it occurs, every active reactor should have an independent international expert team in residence to supervise waste disposal, operational safety, and security/protection from proliferation at that source. The teams should be rotated between countries and report to the Vienna-based International Atomic Energy Agency. Clearly, a new breed of much safer nuclear plants would greatly help to allay the international public's fear of nuclear power.

I have had the opportunity on several occasions to discuss the future of nuclear energy with the co-winner of the 1976 Nobel Prize in Physics, Burton Richter of Stanford University. He sent me a speech he had delivered, where he said: "It is our responsibility, both on ethical grounds and on grounds of self-interest, to develop technologies that will allow the rest of the world to increase their standard of living without at the same time destroying the environment of the planet. I want to turn aside for a moment and express certain bewilderment that I think almost all scientists feel at the opposition to nuclear power by the green movement."

It is encouraging that Patrick Moore, former president of Greenpeace Canada, now supports nuclear energy as an environmentalist.

Risks are an inherent part of decision making in public policy. But the risks must be identified, the risks must be assessed, there must be an application of a cost-benefit analysis to the risks, and, of course, the risks must be managed. So when we look at nuclear energy, it is not a question of saying there is a risk. Of course there are risks, but how do they compare with those of the alternatives? Are we to abandon nuclear energy because of a few accidents? Dams are frequently located upstream from population centres: between 1918 and 1958, thirty-three major dam failures resulted in 1,680 documented fatalities; between 1959 and 1965, nine major dams failed throughout the world. Did we stop building dams as a result? Did we abandon coal because of the high risks associated with coal mining? No. We worked at making technologies more reliable and safety measures stricter.

Unfortunately, much of the public seems either unaware of or unconvinced by the facts. I would go even further: when it comes to the nuclear energy issue, like the issue of genetically modified food, we are in a period where the public is increasingly skeptical of science and of the capacity of governments to create and apply adequate regulatory frameworks for their safety and security.

Perhaps understandably, the public tends to lump all controversial issues involving science into the same basket of suspicion and doubt. Failures to deal adequately with concerns in one area, such as mad cow disease, cascade quickly into others, with the result that facts and sound scientific analysis are often lost in a flood of misperceptions and fears. It is not surprising that politicians give way to these fears or simply refuse to deal with an issue. I would say that refusal to deal with the issue characterizes the nuclear debate in many countries.

The future of energy is not the future of any one part of the globe. It is the future of this fragile planet, the pale blue dot travelling alone through dark, uninhabited space. Our solar system appears to be empty of life except for us. We live on a planet that will survive whatever we do to it, but without the right policies it may not have *Homo sapiens* as a fellow traveller.

Does nuclear energy have a future? It deserves one because it could help to ensure our own.

12

The Scourge of Corruption, Public and Private

For from the least of them even to the greatest of them, Everyone is greedy for gain, And from the prophet even to the priest Everyone deals falsely.

Book of Jeremiah

A May 2016 study by the IMF is headlined "Fighting Corruption Critical for Growth and Macroeconomic Stability." Nothing undermines our democracies and free market economies as much as corruption fed by individual greed.

Corruption is destroying the future of Russia and threatening the future of China, but at least the Chinese leadership recognizes it. Corruption is relegating the poor and uneducated in developing countries to living in poverty and misery while a few of their compatriots bask in the luxury of wealth. In developed countries even legal corruption is undermining the future of open market free enterprise economies through the greed and legal shenanigans of those in a position to game the system, especially in financial services "because that's where the money is," as Willie Sutton famously said. More about that below.

Combating corruption is an ongoing and never-ending challenge. I liken corruption to a chronic disease caused by multiple factors, including poverty, poor political and business leadership, institutional weakness, and of course personal greed for money, power, prestige, and recognition.

We have found no cure for this disease. Uncontrolled, financial corruption paralyzes a country's capacity to efficiently invest capital and penalizes the innocent, especially the poor of the developing world. It is a plague in all countries, especially non-democratic ones. Uncontained, it can shake even healthy democratic institutions.

Nearly all unethical behaviour in business is rooted in individual greed, as in insider trading, which entails enriching oneself at someone else's expense. Where the losers are not readily identifiable, the greedy escape any sense of guilt.

Ethical entrepreneurial businessmen and women risk their own capital to accumulate wealth through creativity and innovation. They are the foundation of successful economic development – the locomotives that generate ever-increasing wealth for society as a whole, with concomitant job creation and tax revenues for the common good.

ILLEGAL AND LEGAL CORRUPTION

Having witnessed ethical and unethical business practices from various perspectives in my professional and public careers, I divide the unethical practices into two categories:

1   unethical practices that are fraudulent and illegal and subject to state-imposed sanctions, often criminal, carrying monetary penalties and possible prison sentences; and
2   unethical practices that are not illegal and for which state-imposed sanctions and penalties do not yet, and may never, exist. For example, in most countries insider trading, now in the first category, used to be in the second. It only moved from the first to the second in the United States in 1934. With both types of unethical practices, a few people enrich themselves at the expense of others.

How can we minimize these practices? For illegal practices the answer is clear: we need to rigorously apply relevant laws and regulations, assuming that an appropriate legal framework exists with supporting public institutions, including an independent, honest, and efficient judicial system. For practices that are unethical but legal, the answer is problematic. Consider the financial debacle that began with the subprime derivative scandals in the United States and ignited a global economic downturn. Were the actions of the financial services community illegal? Perhaps not, but they were clearly unethical.

In the paragraphs below I discuss several examples of unethical practices and suggest how this abstruse area might be addressed. In developing market economies we must be concerned first and foremost about illegal unethical business practices such as corruption, which frequently takes the form of bribes to public officials, often politicians or bureaucrats.

THE ANTI-BRIBERY CONVENTION

I found it personally satisfying to be secretary-general of the OECD when member countries adopted the Convention on Combating Bribery of Foreign Public Officials (known as the Anti-Bribery Convention) in 1997. The Convention supports good corporate governance by penalizing business executives who condone bribery as a commercial practice.

Visiting the OECD for the signing ceremony, US Secretary of State Madeleine Albright made a very positive impression on the ministers in attendance, enhanced no doubt by her ability to address the meeting in French. The Convention was seen as a building block of globalization. It was adopted to support efforts to create a level playing field for fair competition internationally, where the quality of the product and not the size of the bribe would determine the winner. Another important building block that followed soon after was the establishment of international principles for corporate governance.

PRINCIPLES OF CORPORATE GOVERNANCE

The following spring, the OECD members called upon the OECD to develop, in co-operation with national governments, relevant international organizations, regulators, and the private sector, a set of corporate governance principles. These were completed and adopted by the OECD members in early 1999, after broad consultation and input from others, including non-member countries, the World Bank, and the IMF. Because of the broad and inclusive participation in their creation, when the Principles were published in October 1999 they were quickly identified as the world standard.

Soon, however, the world was swept by a series of major corporate scandals, led by the Enron collapse in the United States in 2001 and quickly followed by others, notably the bankruptcy of WorldCom, which proved to be an even larger bankruptcy than Enron's. Countries demanded that the OECD go back to the drawing board with all its collaborators and revise the Principles of Corporate Governance almost before the ink had dried on the first text.

Two acknowledged experts led a task force to revise the Principles. Sir Adrian Cadbury, an accomplished business executive with roots in the family chocolate empire, had authored the famous Cadbury Code of the 1990s, which was a pioneering effort in the area. Ira Millstein, the renowned Wall Street attorney, had a long and successful record pushing for best practices of corporate governance. As a strong advocate of increased director independence, he also championed a greater role for directors sitting on company boards. With Australian ambassador Veronique Ingram, a former senior official from the Australian Treasury, chairing the task force, they produced the first revision in 2004. The scandals that rained down upon us in the early 2000s had moved corporate governance to the centre stage of public policy concerns.

Wednesday, 19 February 2003, was important in furthering the OECD's corporate governance agenda. In the evening I met with a delegation of the NATO Parliamentary Assembly, an inter-parliamentary organization of senior legislators that was in Paris that week to discuss current economic issues. As this was one of the few occasions when a group of prominent US congressmen came to the OECD, I used this opportunity to outline corruption's demoralizing impact on the attitude of investors and the general public and told them about the OECD's work to address this insidious disease by strengthening corporate governance.

Earlier in the day I had met with the French minister of the economy, finance, and industry, Francis Mer. A no-nonsense industrialist turned politician, from 2002 to 2004 Mer was second only to the prime minister as the most powerful person in the French cabinet. He had invited me to meet with him to discuss the progress of work on the revised Principles, which he hoped to be able to report on before the G8 leaders at their forthcoming summit, which France was host-ing in June.

Thanks to Mer's experience in the business world, it was a very useful discussion. The role of directors and the responsibilities and accountability of management were subjects to which he needed no introduction. Some of the unfolding scandals pointed to criminal activity far beyond the scope of good corporate governance alone. But Mer emphasized that when directors do their homework and pay attention, when internal audit mechanisms are robust and the audit committee carefully reviews all relevant materials on a timely basis, and when external auditors are vigilant and truly independent, the scope for management fraud is markedly reduced or entirely elimi-nated. Without those conditions, it is like leaving the safe door open and hoping that no one is tempted to take advantage.

I watched Mer in action at his first International Monetary and Finance Committee (IMFC) and World Bank meeting in Washington in the autumn of 2002. A forceful and forthright businessman who had successfully led steel giant Arcelor during difficult times, Mer was the first business leader since 1958 to hold the challenging economic, finance, and industry portfolio in the French cabinet. Just what was needed, I thought, although politics rarely proves to be a long-term career for a person who dares to call it as he or she sees it. That fate befell Mer. A similar fate awaited former Treasury Secretary Paul O'Neill, Mer's US counterpart for a brief overlapping period. O'Neill, who had been the head of giant aluminum producer Alcoa, was cut from very similar cloth. A straight shooter who exuded honesty and conviction, O'Neill was fired by George W. Bush in December 2002 after disagreements over tax cuts.

Since my arrival at the OECD in 1996, I had dealt with five French ministers of finance, including the charismatic and very capable socialist Dominique Strauss-Kahn, who resigned in 1999 to defend himself against scurrilous accusations from which he was completely exonerated in 2001. His exoneration did not come soon enough to help save the Jospin government from defeat in the spring of 2002. I was probably the only beneficiary of Strauss-Kahn's legal misfor-tunes. For a brief time after his resignation, he served at the OECD as my special advisor, and I appreciated first hand the depth and breadth of his talent.

As we drove up to the ministry to meet Minister Mer, I reflected upon the work the OECD had already done to fight corruption. It had been inspired not by corporate scandals and misbehaviour but by the recognition that in a rapidly globalizing world internationally consistent principles of corporate governance are necessary to attract investment, particularly to developing and emerging market economies.

The OECD Principles stated that the corporate governance framework should ensure the strategic guidance of the company, the effective monitoring of management by the directors, and the accountability of the directors to the company and the shareholders. Directors of some public companies were too often the handmaidens of management, which proposed them for election. Given only information supplied by management, directors were often unaware of the corrupt practices of the corporation until they read about a scandal in the press. We need independent directors with the necessary knowledge, time, and ability to hold management to account.

Unfortunately, our recommendations did not incorporate two principles that history suggests are increasingly important for public companies without a dominant shareholder. They were discussed by the task force but no consensus emerged that would have allowed them to be incorporated into the Principles. First, the chair of the board should be a strong and independent director who holds office for a limited term. The chair should not be the chief executive officer (CEO) or former CEO of the company and should decide what materials are brought before the board of directors in a timely manner. Second, shareholders should approve certain actions by directors, including decisions about the type and level of senior management's remuneration. It was apparent from the task force's discussions that the litmus test for many was the unjustifiable level of executive remuneration, which was a particular problem in the United States and was becoming an issue worldwide.

The impact of the first set of OECD Principles was brought home to me on a visit to Xiamen, China, in 1999 for an investment seminar. The Chinese had published the Principles, noting that they were the accepted global standards.

Principles, as opposed to rules, could assist member and non-member governments to evaluate and improve the legal, institutional, and regulatory frameworks for corporate governance in their countries and provide guidance and suggestions for stock exchanges, investors, corporations, and others interested in developing good corporate governance. The Principles addressed five areas: (1) the rights of shareholders; (2) the equitable treatment of shareholders; (3) the role of stakeholders in corporate governance; (4) disclosure and transparency; and (5) the responsibility of the board of directors to ensure the strategic guidance of the company, the effective monitoring of management by the board, and the board's accountability to the company and to the shareholders.

Although the OECD Principles were designed for a global audience, only 30 countries were members of the OECD. How could we reach the others? The answer was to partner with the World Bank. The bank's president, Jim Wolfensohn, and I had already established a co-operative and friendly relationship and here was yet another area where our two organizations could develop obvious synergies. Jim and I signed an agreement to combine our efforts to encourage developing countries around the world to follow OECD legal and regulatory frameworks for corporate governance. Joint corporate governance round tables brought together regulators, industry, governments, World Bank professionals, and experts including Ira Millstein, Sir Adrian Cadbury, and Peter Dey from Canada. Dey had vast experience not only as a director but also as a former chairman of the Ontario Securities Commission. During his time at the commission it issued the Dey Report on corporate governance entitled "Where Were the Directors?" That question continues to be central to the corporate governance debate.

Round tables were established in Russia, southeastern Europe, South America, and the Far East with a view to improving and reviewing governance in these diverse regions of the world. In this period of rapidly increasing global investment, these markets offered exciting returns, but without robust corporate governance within effective and transparent legal and regulatory frameworks they were unlikely to attract the private capital investment that their economies needed.

Although corporate governance by itself does not address corruption, it does provide mechanisms to minimize opportunities for corruption, a subject I had discussed with Francis Mer. It was also an effective way to build confidence in the rapidly growing emerging economies, which could then attract investments from mutual funds and pension funds, for example, from the OECD area.

As far as I can recall, it did not cross anyone's mind to preach corporate governance to the sophisticated business leaders of the OECD family of countries, and certainly not to American executives. One such executive, when I mentioned that the OECD had engaged Cadbury as a co-chair of a task force on corporate governance, declared to the assembled dignitaries at an exclusive meeting, "Cadbury! What a nuisance." I sensed that his view had considerable support in the meeting.

The series of breathtaking scandals of the early 1990s incited ministers like Francis Mer to push the issue of corporate governance well up their agendas. They sought to strengthen the 1999 version of the Principles. There was good reason for doing this: the succession of revelations shook the foundations of confidence in the governance of major corporations in America, then Europe and elsewhere. Who could be trusted?

The malfeasance that caused the Enron affair was a shock to all, including stockholders and pensioners who saw their savings and security evaporate. Enron was a great American success story and its charismatic leader, Ken Lay, was one of the world's most admired business leaders. Affectionately referred to by George W. Bush as Kenny Boy, he even had the distinction of co-chairing the Republican National Convention in 1992.

Ken Lay was a star performer. At my invitation he attended the OECD Forum in 2000 and we met again at a gathering of the E8 (the world's largest electrical utilities) in Venice. A charming man who made spellbinding presentations on Enron and energy issues, I wondered whether he was really responsible for the Enron debacle or whether Lay was a victim of the machinations of others. The *Economist*, noting his many positive attributes, characterized him as a "good Lay."

Some worried, and with good cause, that the fallout of the Enron affair might have macroeconomic implications as investors lost con-

fidence in financial systems. A senior US congressman, Doug Bereu-
ter of Nebraska, told me that his electors were shocked and did not
know where to turn for advice because the roles of service providers
– analysts, auditors, investment bankers, and even credit rating agencies – seemed to have been compromised by the dramatic events that
continued to unfold around the world. The collapse of Enron, the
fifth largest corporation by capitalization in the United States, caused
many people to question the integrity of equity markets.

BRIBERY FOR PROCUREMENT
AND THE LOCKHEED SCANDAL

In addition to the negative effects of inadequate corporate governance, the OECD also saw international bribery as an impediment to
sound global trade and investment. Corporations from OECD countries
routinely bribed foreign public officials, usually those in developing
countries who handled, or could influence, the award of procurement
contracts in their countries. Within the OECD, bribery that would be
illegal domestically was at least tacitly condoned for businesses selling
in international markets. In some countries, companies were permitted
to treat such bribery payments as deductions for income tax purposes.
This meant that international contracts for products, such as military
equipment or civilian jetliners, were handed out not on the basis of
quality or price but on the size of the bribes.

I was quite familiar with this issue, having represented Lockheed
Aircraft Corporation as Canadian legal counsel in the 1970s when
Lockheed and Boeing were competing to sell long-range patrol aircraft to the Canadian government to provide stronger surveillance
over Canada's extensive coastlines. In early 1976 an infamous scandal
broke, with evidence that Lockheed had bribed a number of prominent
foreign officials in Europe and Asia to advise their governments to buy
Lockheed planes. The US Congress was outraged. Lockheed's chairman, Daniel Haughton, and its president, Carl Kotchian, were both
forced to resign. Robert Haack, former president of the New York
Stock Exchange and a man of impeccable credentials, was appointed
temporary CEO to stem further damage and refurbish the company's

tarnished reputation. Lockheed found itself on the brink of an abyss, and the future of many of its suppliers across the United States was threatened. The collapse of this great company would have resulted in the loss of technology and thousands of jobs.

Lockheed senior management was concerned that the bribery allegations would bias the Canadian government against selecting it. A senior team led by Chairman Haack flew to Ottawa to meet with me and to find out if this important contract would be denied to Lockheed even if the technical representations were supported by the procurement officers and the military. Then something happened that would be impossible in today's new world of professional registered lobbyists. I phoned the prime minister's office and got through to him immediately. He was used to my calls. I was a personal lawyer of the Trudeau family and was frequently in contact with him through his long-time secretary, Mme Viau.

He said that the problem was not the bribery issue, but the large upfront payments that Lockheed required, which exceeded the funding schedule profile of the federal budget. Then, to my surprise, he invited me to come over to his official residence at 24 Sussex for a small dinner: just Trudeau, his guest Buckminster Fuller, and me. Fuller expounded upon a wide range of his theories from architecture to the future of copper, which both Trudeau and I enjoyed (Trudeau was always appreciated as a good listener).

When Fuller left, Trudeau explained why the government's existing budget for the aircraft could not meet the Lockheed cash flow requirements and that the government would not compromise other program spending to do so. This meant that bridge financing would be necessary, which I set about to obtain from Canadian banks. I was surprised that my efforts to obtain such financing, secured by the binding contract covenant of the Canadian federal government, failed. This astonished me given the government's credit rating, but it taught me how stupid some business people become when they have an irrational bias against government. One bank president ruefully said to me, "I do not trust Trudeau." We were ultimately successful with a consortium of US banks led by the Bank of America, and Lockheed won the contract in 1976.

The company emerged from the scandals as one of the great path-finders in American aeronautic and space technology and operates now as Lockheed Martin. I enjoyed working closely in these negotiations to complete the sale to Canada with Roy Anderson, who began as an accountant with the company and rose to be a very successful CEO. He is widely credited with restoring Lockheed to stability and profit.

Canada's business with Lockheed was conducted transparently and under great scrutiny; the contract for the Orion mark long-range patrol aircraft was won on both cost and technical merits. But news of bribes by Lockheed in Europe, the Middle East, and Asia to public officials was followed by evidence that this practice was widespread among US military suppliers. Government concern and public outcry inspired the quick adoption of the US Foreign Corrupt Practices Act (FCPA) in 1977.

Unable to pay bribes, the Americans now found themselves at a disadvantage when competing with other countries for foreign business. In an attempt to remedy this imbalance, the United States initially pressed the OECD to adopt a rather toothless declaration against the bribery of foreign public officials. The text was not supported by some other countries who were undoubtedly pleased with the moral straightjacket the United States had imposed upon itself with the FCPA.

But suddenly, in the late 1990s, there was a sea change. Upping the ante on America's vacuous declaration, the French suggested a legally binding international convention. As the British say, people were gobsmacked. Most perceived the French, along with the Germans, as benefiting from the status quo especially in foreign sales of military hardware and even civilian aircraft. The OECD Anti-Bribery Convention was negotiated in record time.

Pressure from Transparency International and its leader, Peter Eigen, made a huge contribution by exposing the magnitude of the problem and engaging public policy-makers around the globe in this fight against corruption. Eigen knew that the OECD was the logical place to move forward with a binding convention because nearly all "bribers" would be from OECD countries. Many non-members have also joined the Convention, and it remains a landmark in the fight against international corruption.

There was no evidence that a sudden tsunami of moral rectitude swept across the Western industrialized world, so why did so many countries suddenly change their attitudes toward combating corruption? The answer, I believe, is the impact of market globalization. In the 1970s, when the Lockheed scandal broke, countries were protecting their industries, especially their national champions. The Americans did not have one national champion to support and protect; they had several. Lockheed, Boeing, McDonnell Douglas, General Dynamics, and others were going head to head in foreign markets, greasing the palms of politicians and officials who were in a position to demand bribes. The FCPA was perceived as an attempt by the United States to level the playing field among its national companies who were competing with each other for business abroad.

SECRETARY POWELL ON CORRUPTION AND TAXATION

Meeting with Colin Powell at his office in the State Department shortly after he assumed office, I outlined the importance of the Convention and the OECD's follow-up work. He then recounted his experience as an election overseer in a sub-Saharan African country. During a discussion with a local about the candidates, the man declared the entire lot of them to be corrupt. Still, the local said, he had made his choice – on the grounds that at least this particular candidate had a reputation for spending his ill-begotten gains within the country. Powell chuckled as he related this incident, in wry recognition that there was still a very long way to go before corruption could be controlled in many parts of the world.

We had pleasant and wide-ranging discussions on many issues, including the efforts of China to embrace open market economics. Having been impressed with the Chinese leadership's views on these issues during my visit and meetings with ministers and officials in Xiamen and Beijing, I asked whether Powell would soon be visiting in his capacity as the new secretary of state.

"Not until they give me our airplane back," he quickly riposted. This was a reference to a United States Navy spy plane on a routine surveillance mission near the Chinese coast that had collided with a Chinese fighter jet in April 2001 and made an emergency landing in China. The United States sought the return of the crew, who all survived, as well as the aircraft, which was armed with sophisticated intelligence equipment. The crew members were returned quickly but the aircraft not for some months, which is what irritated Powell.

Then Powell leaned back in his chair and asked, "What about taxes?" This came as a surprise for me as he was the secretary of state, not in the Treasury. However, it emerged that he was a major contact point for the so-called black caucus in the US Congress. Those congressmen were apparently the target of lobbying efforts by Caribbean leaders in particular who regarded tax haven income as a critical component of their domestic budgets. The OECD, with its efforts to bring transparency to international taxation and reduce the corruption of tax evasion, was seen as their enemy.

As a former tax lawyer, I had followed the work of the OECD in this area with great interest. I had used tax havens for the benefit of clients in my years as a tax lawyer, especially in the Bahamas and Bermuda. However, I had used them for legal transactions that were fully disclosed to the taxation authorities. This was considered legal tax avoidance.

Tax evasion, by contrast, involves evading the payment of taxes often by relying on bank secrecy protection, which was practised in many jurisdictions, including Switzerland, an important member country of the OECD. Apart from taxation, bank secrecy also accommodated (and accommodates) money flowing from criminal activities, such as the illegal drug trade and money laundering. It is discouraging and demoralizing for honest taxpayers to see Jerome Cahuzac, when he was the budget minister in President Hollande's government in France, charged with initially hiding personal assets in a Swiss bank account and then shifting them to Singapore where it was assumed they would be less likely to be discovered. However, it is expected that he will spend a few years in prison, which should discourage others from following similar criminal practices.

At the OECD our tax committee was supported by a first-class team of experts led by Jeffrey Owens, an energetic and creative tax expert. I made an effort to attend their meetings. It was evident to these country experts that the financial implications for national governments of tax evasion, and perhaps even tax avoidance, were much greater than most politicians and their governments realized. We were to learn in 2016 when the Panama Papers became public that billions and possibly trillions of dollars of revenues might be at stake, to the detriment of ordinary citizens who had neither the financial resources nor the access to expensive expertise to enjoy the advantages afforded to criminals and the famous 1 per cent.

While Secretary Powell was being pressured by the black caucus in Congress to rein in the OECD's activities, I was faced with another constituency seemingly led by the Washington-based Heritage Foundation. It claimed that the OECD, a European-based organization, was striving to create a universal tax system based on the European model, whatever that was. They were pressuring the US Congress to reduce funding to this dangerous European institution.

This became a tense and challenging issue, in part because of our own communication failures. We had introduced our examination of all these tax regimes, supported by bank secrecy, under a program named "Harmful Tax Competition." That was seized upon by the Heritage Foundation as proof that the OECD was against tax competition and therefore favouring tax uniformity in line with the alleged European model.

I had learned from my experience in the Canadian federal cabinet that no policy should be released without a communication strategy. This had not been happening in Canada, so the prime minister added a valuable cabinet member who had the necessary background to ensure that a communication strategy was put into place before any policy was released.

I carried that lesson to the OECD, where I brought an extremely astute communications person into our weekly strategy sessions. Chris Brooks identified the problem with the title our committee had assigned to our important tax work, which risked being sabotaged by the lobbying of the Heritage Foundation. Senator Judd Greg from New Hampshire was even threatening to block the US funding for the OECD, since his state benefited from no sales tax. Any prospect of tax uniformity was an anathema to him.

"Tax competition is what many of our members want," Chris Brooks declared. "We are really shooting ourselves in the foot with this description of OECD work on taxation."

Of course he was right. We changed the name of the project to "Harmful Tax Practices," and the objections subsided.

Of course few US senators agreed with shutting down the United States' financial contribution to the OECD on this issue. I raised this on several occasions with Senator John McCain, who always struck me as having a thoughtful and sensible view. He said, "Don't worry too much; that will not happen."

In fact, the OECD's work in this area is now much appreciated, especially by the G20, largely because there is more knowledge about the vast sums being held in tax havens that should be contributing to the growth of domestic economies. The OECD's work highlighted another example of greed over good. It also served as a lesson in ensuring that policies are properly communicated so as to be easily understood by target audiences, in this case the US Congress, which supported about 25 per cent of the OECD budget.

My successor, Angel Gurría, now has another issue to deal with that illustrates the ingenuity of the accounting and legal professions. In my time we were primarily focused on tax evasion and bank secrecy. Tax avoidance was also being dealt with, primarily through domestic laws to close legal loopholes.

In recent years, tax engineers have developed sophisticated mechanisms that place intellectual property rights in tax-free jurisdictions and then license their use to franchise holders in different countries, including members of the OECD. This enables royalties to be paid out to affiliated companies in tax havens where the funds are used for further offshore investment or remitted on favourable terms through tax treaty networking to the ultimate beneficiary, normally a major multinational.

Known as base erosion and profit shifting (BEPS), thanks to the work of the OECD, it has become a major focus of the G20. This successful history of exposing and suggesting remedies to control international tax evasion and avoidance schemes should make a generous contribution to the treasuries of many countries and result in a fairer sharing of the tax burden.

I explained the importance of the OECD tax work to Secretary Powell, although the challenge of BEPS was to come many years later. He appeared to listen carefully, and undoubtedly the Enron scandal and bankruptcy later in the year, which exposed Enron's web of offshore affiliates, must have added much credibility to and support for the OECD's tax work. The secretary and I then returned to the question of bribery and the Convention signed by his predecessor, Madeleine Albright.

The OECD Convention was a start, but restricting the bribery of public officials is not sufficient. Bribery and corruption can pervert the procurement process when many sectors – utilities and transportation, including airlines – are increasingly being privatized. Surely this Convention or another should be extended to private corruption and not just that of public officials. In addition, the United States' lead negotiator on the Convention, the State Department's Al Larson, who was a former US ambassador to the OECD, had argued for the inclusion of legislators in the definition of public officials. This suggestion was rejected by European interests.

Sadly, there is also evidence that a large portion of official development aid is diverted through corruption in recipient countries. Unfortunately the Convention does not cover such despicable, criminal activities; any appropriate recourse is often dependent on the very dishonest politicians and officials through whom such aid passes.

According to UN Secretary-General Ban Ki-moon, a study has shown that not less than 30 per cent of foreign aid never reaches its intended destination. Total foreign aid in 2015 (the last number available at the time of writing) was US$135.94 billion, so some US$40 billion of that probably found its way into the personal treasuries of unworthy officials and despots who are enriching themselves at the expense of their own people. These criminals, and the bankers who facilitate secret accounts and schemes, are stealing the education, health care, and jobs of the very people they are meant to protect.

How can we cure the public sector corruption that is undermining good government, destroying public confidence in democratic institutions, and denying the benefits of competitive free trade by making the size of the bribe more important than the price and quality of the product?

How do we know that global corruption is thriving? Our best source of information is Transparency International, which has developed credible surveys to measure a country's level of corruption. A Transparency International progress report on enforcement of the OECD Convention, covering forty-one countries, shows that there are four countries with active enforcement, six with moderate enforcement, nine with limited enforcement, and twenty with little or none. Two were not classified. Choking off the supply side of bribery should in theory dry up the demand side from dishonest politicians and bureaucrats in client countries. Alas, this is good in theory but less effective in practice, particularly as the world's second-largest economy, China, has not signed the Convention.

SOME SUGGESTED APPROACHES

To control the scourge of corruption, I offer the following propositions.

Proposition 1

All levels of government – national, regional, and municipal – must be free of corruption so that corporations cannot find a crack through which to pour their bribes. It is difficult, if not impossible, to have an ethical business community in a country with a corrupt government. Companies dependent upon such governments for concessions, infrastructure contracts, import and export permits, licences, and privileges to operate need to pay bribes to do business.

It is not just a moral issue. Though countries that tolerate high levels of corruption usually have difficulty attracting foreign direct investment, oil, gas, and mining investments must go where the resource is located. Hence resource-rich nations such as Kazakhstan, Russia, and numerous African countries are high on the Transparency International corruption scale because companies are often forced to pay bribes to obtain permits and concessions.

Companies based in OECD countries that adhere to the OECD

Anti-Bribery Convention will continue to be at a competitive disadvantage opposite those in countries such as China that continue to consider bribery of foreign officials to be an acceptable practice. In 2013, when the Chinese equivalent of the Fortune 500 largest Chinese corporations invited me to speak about the deleterious effects of public sector corruption on economic and social progress, I saw a glimmer of hope that with his national anti-corruption campaign President Xi might be convinced to sign and enforce the OECD Convention. It has not happened yet.

Proposition 2

All legal means available must be used to root out corruption by public officials, allowing business to operate in a transparent competitive environment without bribes or intimidation.

I focus on China because its behaviour will have a huge impact on how the global commercial world governs itself when it soon becomes the world's largest economy. In November 2012, the past Chinese president, Hu Jintao, told the 18th National Congress as he left office that addressing illegal corruption among public officials is high on China's public policy agenda. He said:

> Combating corruption and promoting political integrity, which is a major political issue of great concern to the people, is a clear-cut and long-term political commitment of the Party. If we fail to handle this issue well, it could prove fatal to the Party, and even cause the collapse of the Party and the fall of the state. Leading officials at all levels, especially high-ranking officials, must readily observe the code of conduct on clean governance and report all important matters. They should both exercise strict self-discipline and strengthen education and supervision over their families and their staff; and they should never seek any privilege.

President Xi is reinforcing that message, as seen in this Bloomberg report (4 March 2014): "President Xi Jinping's campaign against corruption is growing into one of the broadest in China's modern history, snaring dozens of businessmen and government officials ...

Xi, who became president last year, is trying to unwind a culture of bribery and graft that has hurt the government's legitimacy and jeopardized economic growth."

Some people ask whether the Chinese government uses charges of corruption to eliminate political opponents. I had numerous occasions to meet with the charismatic Bo Xilai, the extremely popular princeling and governor of Liaoning. Destined to become a member of the politburo, he was instead charged with corruption and put under house arrest, to remove him from the political process. Whether this action was politically motivated remains a question in many minds because corruption appears to be deeply rooted and widespread in the Chinese culture, and it may serve as a quick and convenient way to sideline political opponents. According to a report in the *Globe and Mail* (2 August 2014), "corruption in China dates back thousands of years, a fact of life in the various imperial dynasties – much as it was in many Western monarchies throughout history."

Perhaps things are changing. More optimistically, the coverage of a politburo meeting by Hong Kong's *Ming Pao* newspaper notes that "Xi Jinping made points on three anti-corruption issues: First, someone inside the party said that authorities arrested over 30 Vice Minister cadres after the 18th National Congress and that this should be good enough and the anti-corruption effort should stop. Xi Jinping is said to have replied saying this is a wrong understanding, and that there is no quota for the anti-corruption effort. Xi said they should arrest however many are corrupt." Xi understands that honest public officials cannot be bribed and that dishonest public officials not only accept bribes but demand bribes and routinely do so in many non-OECD countries.

Proposition 3

To avoid corrupt practices, make sure that public servants are incorruptible.

Through my experience as a Canadian cabinet member responsible for the national public service and as OECD's secretary-general I have met with public service officials across the globe and I have become convinced that a highly trained, well-remunerated, dedicated, and honest public service is the only way to ensure honest, effective, and competent public and private sectors.

To provide a steady stream of high-quality public servants to administer the entire machinery of government, including the judicial system, every country should have programs to train managers from each level of government. Those privileged to attend should commit to the public service for a number of years so that quality personnel, developed at taxpayer expense, are not poached immediately by the private sector.

To draw an analogy from the world of computers, these highly trained public servants represent the operating systems. The institutions, courts, administrative tribunals, army, and police represent the hardware of government and the political class should bring the policy options – the software – to be introduced to the operating system, that is, the public service. Corruption in the public service is analogous to a serious virus in your computer. No government can effectively forward its social and economic agendas without a first-class public service.

Proposition 4

Governments must apply the laws and quash illegal corruption in the public and private sectors without bias or discrimination.

Even in the United States, the difference between legal and illegal corruption often seems lost in a flood of revelations about corporate malfeasance: insider trading (illegal); the repugnant activities of well-known banks and investment banks who duped uninformed investors into purchasing instruments secured by the equivalent of financial garbage (perhaps legal); or money laundering and aiding and abetting massive tax evasion (illegal). The fines imposed run into many billions of dollars but the individual corporate bureaucrats responsible have so far largely avoided criminal or even civil penalties. There are suggestions they may yet face penalties, which would be a very good thing.

In 2014 the Bank of America settled its case with the US government by paying a $16.5 billion fine, and in early 2016 Goldman Sachs was fined $5.1 billion. These huge settlements are part of a series totaling more $50 billion. US Attorney General Eric Holder and several state attorneys general issued a statement on the settlement on 24 August 2014 (US Department of Justice news release 14-884). It contained these paragraphs on the fraudulent practices surrounding the sale of residential-mortgage backed securities (RMBS):

> "Today's settlement attests to the fact that fraud pervaded every level of the RMBS industry, including purportedly prime securities, which formed the basis of our filed complaint," said U.S. Attorney Anne M. Tompkins for the Western District of North Carolina. "Even reputable institutions like Bank of America caved to the pernicious forces of greed and cut corners, putting profits ahead of their customers. As we deal with the aftermath of the financial melt down and rebuild our economy, we will hold accountable firms that contributed to the economic crisis. Today's settlement makes clear that my office will not sit idly while fraud occurs in our backyard."
>
> The settlement includes a statement of facts, in which the bank has acknowledged that it sold billions of dollars of RMBS without disclosing to investors key facts about the quality of the securitized loans. When the RMBS collapsed, investors, including federally insured financial institutions, suffered billions of dollars in losses.

Despite the attorney general's condemnation and the extraction of $16.5 billion in fines at the expense of the shareholders, we have yet to see any individuals at banks prosecuted criminally for these acts. Unsurprisingly, this has enraged shareholders and others who have suffered heavy financial losses, often including the loss of their homes, while the corporate bureaucrats directly responsible have escaped by paying enormous fines with other people's money. This is unacceptable and is destroying confidence in the integrity of the much-vaunted American model.

Contrast the lack of prosecutions of people in the financial sector with the Enron debacle, where some 16 former executives, including CEO Jeff Skilling, were sentenced to jail time. In that case, as in Martha Stewart's conviction for insider trading, the law was applied without discrimination and justice was done. Is justice being done in the financial sector cases, in a country proud to declare that it applies fairly the rule of law?

As I told my Chinese audience in 2014, I hope that developing and emerging markets expanding their financial sectors will contain illegal corruption by applying the law without discrimination.

Proposition 5

The widening income gap between senior executives and their average workers is not illegal, but it is immoral and unsustainable.

Though the board of directors, usually through a remuneration committee, approves the remuneration packages of senior executives, legal corruption is an appropriate classification for this practice. Directors are usually under management's influence, and remuneration committees are often composed of senior executives from other corporations. This situation lends itself to mutual back-scratching and probably accounts for the outrageous growth of executive pay; these pay increases have not trickled down to the average worker in the United States and elsewhere.

Too often corporate managers don't see themselves as stewards of other peoples' money but as partners entitled to huge "entrepreneurial" rewards for doing what they are already extremely well paid to do. They expect generous stock options that will catch the tide of rising values on the stock exchange with no comparable downside risk, as well as outsized salaries and bonuses bearing no relationship to value for money.

In 2003, William McDonough, then chairman of the Federal Reserve Bank of New York and an expert on corporate governance, spoke out against such executive behaviour in a speech at a September 11 commemorative service at Trinity Church. He pointed out that in 1980 the average large-company CEO made 40 times more than the firm's average worker. By 2000 that multiple had risen to about 400 times. He said, "I should also note that I knew a lot of CEOs in 1980, and I can assure you that the CEOs of 2000 were not ten times better – if any better at all ... The reason for the outrageous disparities between the wages of workers and executives is the widespread executive greed and the cooking-the-books phenomenon. The people thought that the business leadership in general needed a sharp lesson."

That lesson took the form of the onerous legislation of the Sarbanes–Oxley Act of 2002. These abuses brought much public anger about corporate governance, and as McDonough has said, the politicians listened. Is it not that same anger that gave rise to the Occupy Wall Street movement and into which Senator Bernie Sanders tapped so effectively during the 2016 Democratic primaries?

Unfortunately, individual greed continues unabated, as reported in USA Today on 4 April 2014: "USA Today's analysis of Standard & Poor's 500 companies headed by the same CEO the past two fiscal years shows 2013 median pay … jumped 13% to $10.5 million … Coming in a year in which corporate earnings gains continue to come mostly from job cuts and streamlining instead of organic growth, as well as nearly a decade of stagnant wage growth for rank-and-file workers, continued gains in CEO pay underscore the disconnect between boardrooms and Main Street. Among the nation's 104.8 million full-time workers, average median annual wages were $40,872 last year, up just 1.4% over 2012."

Corrective action is overdue. A first and simple step would be to require executive remuneration, bonuses, and stock options to be approved at the annual shareholder meeting.

Proposition 6

Legal corruption by corporate executives is damaging the integrity of free markets and the health of economies and should be made illegal through the application of either principles or rules.

The actions of bankers selling financial instruments that they knew to be overvalued and toxic is one example of this corruption. In some cases, such as at the Bank of America, one would anticipate criminal charges to be laid given the attorney general's declaration that bankers acted knowingly, routinely, falsely and fraudulently. In other cases, behaviour was unethical and immoral but not criminal per se.

The financial sector has been reaping massive rewards through non-productive activities such as securitizing and selling overvalued debt-backed securities.

Noting his disapproval of this practice, John Plender of the *Financial Times*, a participant in the OECD 2004 working group on Principles of Corporate Governance, cited an 1893 comment by Karl Marx: "To the possessor of money capital, the process of production appears merely as an unavoidable intermediate link, as a necessary evil for the sake of money-making. All nations with a capitalist mode of production are therefore seized periodically by a feverish attempt to make money without the intervention of the process of production." Does this sound familiar?

In OECD countries the laws against insider trading, first adopted in the United States in 1934 after the 1929 market crash, brought an end to one great source of wealth for many. Insider trading had always been unethical and wrong and now it was finally illegal. Are we not faced with a similar situation today? Should we not move some actions from the legal but immoral category to the illegal classification?

Proposition 7

To maintain dynamic and creative financial service sectors, governing laws and regulations should be based on principles, with rules used as examples flowing from them.

Lawyers and other professionals are trained to wriggle around rules but cannot escape the application of principles. However, this means entrusting more power to an independent and respected judicial system.

The Lehman Brothers debacle serves as a good example. Following the firm's collapse the examiner's report concluded that executives were involved in "balance sheet manipulation" by implementing an arcane accounting procedure called Repo 105, which masked the bank's true financial condition from investors and regulators, effectively keeping $50 billion of liabilities off its balance sheet. Lehman, apparently unable to get an opinion from an American law firm approving this mechanism, found a UK firm willing to give a favourable opinion and was thereby able to deceive investors and others about the true financial state of the company. Protected by an opinion that permitted such unethical behaviour, the perpetrators of this scheme probably found comfort in its supposed legality.

As rules are clearly not working, is it not time to invoke principles that might govern the behaviour of management? Two come to mind: the principle of transparency and the fiduciary principle, which would require management to act in the best interests of shareholders and other stakeholders such as creditors and employees.

No court of law could have supported Lehman's accounting sleight of hand as fulfilling either principle. The executives who approved it might have thought twice had they known there were criminal consequences attached to such chicanery.

However, with the adoption of the Dodd–Frank Wall Street Reform and Consumer Protection Act, US legislators seem determined to make the rule book even thicker. It is noteworthy that the volume of laws in the US financial sector has expanded dramatically since the 32-page Federal Reserve Act of 1913 and the 37-page Glass–Steagall Act after the Wall Street crash. The recent Dodd–Frank Act is 848 pages long. It is a cash cow for lawyers and accountants but a costly bureaucratic nightmare for business.

Emerging markets trying to build robust financial sectors should carefully assess the costs and benefits of embarking on the "road of rules" being followed in the United States and consider establishing governing principles, with rules flowing from them.

I am told that a very successful and respected Canadian bank president, Cedric Ritchie, when looking at the Sarbanes–Oxley legislation, said something like this: "The problem with these young smart bankers is that they spent too much time in business school and not enough time in Sunday school."

Proposition 8

The judicial system must be totally independent and manned with well-paid justices who are acknowledged by the legal profession and the general public to be highly skilled and of unimpeachable integrity.

Proposition 9

The board of directors should be the guardian of good corporate governance and the interests of shareholders.

The OECD Principles state: "The corporate governance framework should ensure the strategic guidance of the company, the effective

monitoring of management by the board, and the board's accountability to the company and the shareholders."

This points to the need for independent directors with the necessary knowledge, time, and ability to hold management to account.
The starting point, as McDonough suggested, should be to strengthen
the role and independence of outside directors.

Separating the roles of CEO and chair of the board is an increasingly common practice, and it is obligatory in the United Kingdom.
To further guarantee independence, the chair should not come from
the executive group of the company itself, although that is not obligatory in the United Kingdom.

The obvious advantage of separating the functions is that the chair
can demand that relevant information be put before the board. This
prevents management from manipulating the board by drowning a
minimum of relevant data in a maximum number of complicated
pages that directors do not have time to read.

CAPITALISM AND ITS BENEFITS AT RISK

To conclude, if we are to ensure good corporate governance and
contain corruption, both public and private, we must look far
beyond individual scandals or excessive executive compensation to
what is truly at stake: the health of the market economies that have
delivered prosperity and raised standards of living. Corruption and
abuse by corporate bureaucrats have put good capitalism and its
benefits at risk.

What example are we setting for emerging markets like Russia
or China, which we hoped would become robust democracies and
dynamic open market economies by benefiting from the experience
and the practices of OECD economies, notably that of United States?

In the spring of 2005 I sat with William McDonough, Jim Wolfensohn, Ira Millstein, Peter Dey, and other experts at a corporate governance event in Moscow. The conference room at the Marriott Hotel
was filled to capacity. Prime Minister Mikhail Fradkov, Russian businessmen, professionals, regulators, observers, and journalists listened
politely to our wisdom and advice. Given the spate of scandals in OECD

member countries I wondered what they were thinking about the lessons we offered. Perhaps a Russian proverb equivalent to "Physician, heal thyself"? Those sentiments were surely reinforced in the wake of the 2007–08 global financial crisis, another Wall Street export.

13

Shaping Globalization: Dogged by Failure

Addressing the World Trade Organization (WTO) in Singapore in 1996, I wanted to deliver a strong message on the benefits of a globalized world. After hearing a stream of repetitive speeches that ministers felt obliged to deliver, which were too long, boring, and full of well-worn platitudes about the benefits of trade liberalization, I wanted to break the mold. Pointing to the window of opportunity that the creation of the WTO at the Uruguay Round opened to the world, I invoked Shakespeare: "There is a tide in the affairs of men, which, taken at the flood, leads on to fortune; omitted, all the voyage of their life is bound in shallows and in miseries."

Newly arrived as secretary-general of the OECD, perhaps I was somewhat naïve, but as an ardent free trader, the only Liberal member of the Canadian Parliament to vote for the Free Trade Agreement with the United States, I believed that to be true. We appeared to have moved into a new world of international trade and investment that held great promise for global economic growth and development, especially in emerging market economies and developing countries.

I shared my optimism with this gathering of influential ministers and leaders of international organizations:

As the 20th century recedes into history, its twilight years will be characterized by a word or a phrase that will carry a multitude of images, lessons, and historical memories. The Dark Ages, the Renaissance, and the Industrial Revolution are examples. And I would suggest that the end of the twentieth century and the beginning of the twenty-first will be characterized as the dawn of the Age of Globalization.

When historians write of this period there will be a magnificent story to tell: how world leaders harnessed unprecedented opportunities, not just for the developed world, but for the whole global community; how poverty, misery, and disease in the developing world were put on a fast track to eradication through multilateral free trade and investment; how the prosperity of the developed world was sustained through the evolution of the global market; how economic growth was firmly established in the developing world through the adoption of liberal market reforms supported by the transfer of capital, technology, and know-how, combined with unfettered access for their goods and services to the markets of the developed world; how the widening gap between the rich and the poor in the world community was arrested and then began to narrow; and how economic growth and protection of the environment were married forever in pursuit of long-term sustainable development.

Twenty years later that great story has yet to be written and will not be until we do a better job of shaping globalization. The Doha Development Round of WTO negotiations, launched in 2001, failed to provide the hoped-for global free trade framework. True, we have globally reaped enormous benefits from liberalized trade and investment, but the dream I described remains a shadow on a distant horizon, especially the prospect of third world development.

SHOES, UBER, AND GENETICALLY MODIFIED FOODS

A plethora of vested economic interests, sometimes supported by single-interest NGOs, wield increasing political clout, knowing that the short-term election or re-election imperative always prevails. Too rarely do we hear of the enormous benefits that liberalized trade has brought to individual consumers and households. Yet, as Alan Greenspan often pointed out, the price and quality of Chinese imports have helped importing countries to keep inflation low.

This resistance to liberalized trade is not new. The famous nineteenth century American journalist Ambrose Bierce defined a tariff as "a tax on imports, designed to protect the domestic producer against the greed of his consumer." It is not that simple, but Bierce (sometimes known as Bitter Bierce) did put his finger on the most obvious of vested interests resisting trade liberalization and globalization.

I use the phrase "shaping globalization" to describe a process that integrates markets globally as they have generally been integrated nationally through mobility of labour, free trade in goods and services, and the efficient allocation of capital, all underpinned by effective competition policy. It has begun, but it remains a work in progress. Even many domestic markets require important structural reforms to make them operate fairly and efficiently.

In recent years we have seen a major focus on regulatory reform, which has contributed to better functioning markets by encouraging competition in sectors previously protected through state-sanctioned monopolies. Telecommunications, electricity, gas distribution, and transportation come to mind.

RISING TIDES SHOULD LIFT ALL BOATS, NOT JUST YACHTS

Internationally, why are we seeing so much vocal and sometimes violent resistance to global trade and investment liberalization? Studies by the OECD and many others illustrate beyond doubt the immense benefits that have flowed to countries that have opened their markets, as the United Kingdom did in the nineteenth century. So why are people not encouraging politicians to open their markets more quickly?

Trade and investment liberalization have produced substantial increases in the GDP of our societies; better prices for consumers; and more wealth for investors, producers, and wage earners. As Winston Churchill is reported to have said, "Markets are like parachutes. They work best when open."

Yet many in our societies are justifiably fearful of the impacts on employment security, particularly for the traditional production jobs filled by low-skilled and poorly educated people. This appears to be one constituency that President Trump targeted during the 2016 presidential election campaign. That resistance cannot be washed away by lauding the overall societal benefits of free trade. My first-hand political experience helped me to understand the dimensions of that problem and to challenge theoretical economists, many of whom seem to have no sense of the powerful forces of the "political economy" in democratic countries. I turn to that experience below. But first, it is worth noting an opinion piece by George Will in the *Washington Post* (28 December 2016). He opens with this: "It is axiomatic that if someone is sufficiently eager to disbelieve something, there is no Everest of evidence too large to be ignored. This explains today's revival of protectionism, which is a plan to make America great again by making it 1953 again." He provides some challenging statistics for free trade disbelievers, some of which are referenced below.

My own exposure to this challenge was in the early 1980s, when the Trudeau government in Canada recognized that certain sectors of our economy could only exist behind tariff walls that punished consumers with high prices and deprived developing countries of export opportunities. As the minister responsible for economic and regional development, I had a particular interest in this issue.

We planned to adjust three sectors: shoes, clothing, and textiles. Under the plan we would phase out of tariffs over seven years; substantially fund capital investment that would allow industries to modernize and compete with imports; and allocate attractive incentives encouraging new industries to set up in areas where inefficient plants could not survive in the face of foreign competition.

The program was placed under the watchful eye of the late Paul Desmarais, Sr., one of Canada's pre-eminent and most successful business leaders, who was one of the first Canadians to identify and pursue investment opportunities in China. With his interest and experience he was the ideal person to oversee this ambitious program.

On paper it all seemed to make good sense, until I went with Alain Tardif, a fellow Member of Parliament, to a town he represented. The principal industry in Richmond, Quebec, was a primitive, labour-intensive shoe manufacturing operation that could never compete with Asian imports. The average education level of its workers was very low, far from secondary level, as I recall.

What I learned during that visit served as an important lesson. Our proposed program meant that many of those plant workers were going to lose their jobs. Investing capital on modern manufacturing with robotics would require fewer unskilled workers, and it would be hard for those laid off to find jobs in the new high-tech industries we wished to attract.

Think of the political dilemma faced by Alain Tardif, a competent and dedicated Member of Parliament. Clearly the workers in the plant would not welcome the program, and they had votes. Other businesses that supplied goods and services to the shoe manufacturer would also fight the policy, as would their employees, and they also had votes. The owners of that shoe manufacturing facility would prefer to continue to prosper behind a tariff wall without further capital investment, and they provided financial support to the political parties.

Our plan seemed a political non-starter, yet economically it was clearly the right thing to do. It is a good example of the challenges of the political economy where the right economic policy clashes with political electoral imperatives. Alain Tardif's riding was one of a very few non-urban ridings that stayed with our Liberal Party in the next national election. But I am sure our policy did not contribute to his success.

My visit to Richmond confirmed my view that adjustment requires a broad, all-encompassing approach so that workers in all countries do not see their futures swept away by international competition. Even then, many elected politicians will resist putting their careers on the line by supporting unpopular but correct economic policies.

In many ways, new technologies, notably information and communication technologies and their applications, shared worldwide are major contributors to global trade in goods and services but also the displacement of workers in developed economies. Think of Amazon, or the extraordinary international expansion of the Uber taxi service (which illustrates the power of new ways to communicate), or the number of times we talk to a bank teller instead of pushing buttons on an ATM.

Arriving in Paris on a flight from Vienna in the summer of 2015, I found that taxi drivers were on strike, protesting the arrival of Uber, the new evolution in personal transportation. I decided to take the local train from the station at Charles de Gaulle Airport and lugged my heavy baggage down to the airport's train station only to learn that service had been suspended because people were on the tracks (protesting taxi drivers, I presumed). In addition, there had been violent confrontations between taxi and Uber personnel, with a number of Uber cars attacked and burned.

The concierge at the airport Sheraton Hotel came to my rescue with a motorcycle taxi, where I was perched with luggage on a seat behind the skilled driver. Though expensive, it provided me with an unforgettable experience, a curious mixture of fear and excitement as we threaded our way at 120 km/hour between trucks, buses, and cars in heavy rush-hour traffic. It was a once-in-a-lifetime experience and at moments I thought it would surely be my last one.

The French government declared aspects of Uber to be illegal, acceding once again to "government by protest and violence." As a former politician I was very sensitive to the government's dilemma and to the plight of taxi drivers, who would see their investments in taxi medallions (licences) plummet with the arrival of Uber.

At the OECD we consistently preached that public policy must address the losers in free trade, such as traditional taxi drivers, ensuring that they have the skills necessary to participate in the new knowledge economy and that older workers have appropriate support for transition to retirement. Job losses because of technology may prove to be an even more difficult challenge in the years ahead than the migration of businesses to jurisdictions with low-cost labour.

THE INDUSTRIAL REVOLUTION, NED LUDD, AND INFORMATION AND COMMUNICATION TECHNOLOGIES – SAME PSYCHOLOGY

The speed of the job losses due to fast-changing technologies is breathtaking, with the rapid expansion of Uber, which exploits instant electronic communication systems, being an example. New technologies and concomitant job losses have had opponents dating back to 1779, when Ned Ludd allegedly broke new equipment in the textile industry. That experience was being repeated more than 200 years later by the neo-Luddite taxi drivers in Paris.

Reputable studies show that since 1790 new technologies have more than replaced the jobs they made obsolete. But workers who lost jobs in earlier centuries, especially in agriculture, benefited from new ones created in emerging urban manufacturing centres.

In the past, workers had time to prepare because major changes took years to materialize. Not so today. The speed of technologi-cal advancement and the ensuing elimination of traditional jobs are major challenges facing this generation. Although some manufactur-ing is returning to developed countries from developing countries with lower labour costs, technological advances have reduced the number of jobs returning and increased productivity.

President Trump declares that jobs have been stolen from America through stupid trade deals that his predecessors entered into. China and Mexico are prime targets of his vitriol. The president seems to never be inhibited by facts. The George Will commentary I referred to above tells us of credible studies that illustrate that "of the 5.6 million manufacturing jobs lost (in the USA) between 2000 and 2010, trade accounted for 13 percent of job losses and productivity improvements accounted for more than 85 percent."

A study by consultants at Deloitte looked at the impact of technol-ogy on the economy of work in the United Kingdom between 1871 and 2011. The researchers, as reported by the *Guardian*, found that technology has broadly been a "job-creating machine." However, those who have lost jobs are unlikely to have the skills to fill the jobs created in other areas.

Governments often step in when businesses and individuals affected negatively by international competition quite rightly see it as a personal cost to them and are unable to appreciate or bene-fit directly from the advantages accruing to other sectors or society at large. When the second Bush administration imposed high tar-iffs on steel imports, approximately 10,000 jobs were saved in the steel industry, but at a cost of $400,000 per job. And the knock-on effect was the loss of approximately 80,000 jobs in other industries that were forced to buy more expensive steel. In his *Washington Post* opinion piece George Will references former protectionist policies in the United States that were designed to protect screw and bolt manufacturers, the auto sector, and the tire industry, with each such measure usually costing hundreds of millions of taxpayers' dollars. Will concludes, "The past is prologue. The future probably will feature many more such self-defeating government interventions."

President Trump raised expectations of jobs returning in the US steel sector. It will be impressive to see if he can deliver on that promise without creating the disruption and costs experienced in the past.

Globalization in both trade and investment are not new phenomena. When I consulted *The World Economy: A Millennial Perspective* by Angus Maddison, I found that the Netherlands had many thousands of merchant ships – far more than any other country – plying the seven seas in the seventeenth century. Though global market integration in that epoch and into the nineteenth century was not as we see it today, the amount of robust international trade and investment taking place almost 300 years ago comes as a surprise to those who see globalization as a new development.

Maddison reminds us that the United Kingdom, the leading capitalist country of the nineteenth century, followed a policy of zero tariffs and imposed the same policy on others. At the same time, it opened its economy to agricultural imports and watched its own agricultural sector and associated employment wither away.

To a large extent, the United Kingdom had embarked upon global market integration, but within a colonial context. Maddison cites an 1865 quote by British economist Stanley Jevons, who extolled the benefits of free trade for his country: "The plains of North America and Russia are our cornfields; Chicago and Odessa are our granaries; Australasia contains our sheep farms, the Hindus and the Chinese grow tea for us. And our coffee, sugar and spice plantations are in all the Indies."

However, the concept of free trade and globalization is not just an extension of what the world has experienced for centuries. The differences are profound, not only because of the real integration of world markets but also because of shifting sources of production, the evolution of multinational enterprises, and the arrival of information and communication technology systems including the World Wide Web. These developments, coupled with massive transportation networks by sea and air, have brought us to the realization of Marshall McLuhan's global village. Once thought to be a cliché, it is now a reality.

International trade by the colonial powers brought raw materials to Europe where they were converted into finished products either for domestic consumption of for export. Textiles, clothing, and footwear are good examples: the manufacturing of these products in the United Kingdom largely replaced agricultural employment.

Today, such finished products are produced in and imported from all over the planet, usually by multinational enterprises taking advantage of competitive labour costs in developing countries. Components are often sourced in one developing country and final assembly is done in another. As a result, an astonishingly high percentage of imports and exports are intra-firm.

The Internet has added another dimension to the trade in services, with many activities now outsourced to skilled workers in the developing world. India is a major beneficiary of this trend.

The integration of international markets will continue. While high-income developed countries have led the way in expanding trade and investment, the experience of low-income and middle-income countries is mixed. For example, China and many other Asian countries have entered world markets much more successfully than Latin American and African countries. The death of the Doha Development Round of WTO negotiations, intended to help developing countries integrate into the global economy as quickly as possible, is denying economic growth and wealth creation to those who need it most.

The impact of free trade on jobs is not just in the manufacturing sector. The arrival of genetically modified organisms (GMOs) has faced strong protectionist pressure in the agricultural sectors of developed countries. Is the resistance of some countries, such as France, to GMO imports designed to protect French health or French farmers?

In late June 1999 I received a call from Al Larson of the US State Department. He was attending the G7 Summit in Cologne, where participants were discussing the pros and cons of genetically modified crops. He asked me whether the OECD in any of its many areas of work was familiar with issues surrounding genetically modified crops.

I checked and to my surprise, I learned that relevant work was being done by our environment and science and technology directorates. The OECD role in the genetically modified food debate was to supply objective scientific expertise and research to enable countries to come to their own independent judgments. These many years later, possible health concerns as well as the influence of vested trade and agricultural interests remain controversial.

Returning from the G7 Summit, President Chirac took a personal interest in the subject and invited me to discuss the question with him directly at his Élysée office in July. While I had met him at many formal events and receptions, this was my first lengthy one-on-one discussion with the president. I brought our respected and knowledgeable director of agriculture, Gérard Viatte, with me, because I suspected much of the exchange might focus on European protectionism in the agricultural sector. Viatte had worked closely with the trade directorate on these issues.

I found President Chirac well informed, open minded, and candid in expressing concerns about GMO products that the Americans were eager to sell in Europe. However, while the trade issue and the potential vulnerability of the French farmers seemed obvious and were no doubt very important politically to the president, he repeatedly invoked the "principe de précaution" (precautionary principle) as the fundamental concern. This clearly threw the issue into the health arena.

I undertook to press forward with our work, including broad public consultation. The first step was to determine whether to that date there had been any evidence anywhere of GMOs being responsible for negative health impacts.

Upon returning to the OECD I gathered my management team around the conference table in my office to report the results of my meeting with the president. Among those present was Jacques Delors, a former minister of finance in the Mitterrand government and more recently the much-respected head of the European Commission. I was pleased to have been able to enlist him as a personal advisor; such a knowledgeable, experienced, modest, and agreeable person would be hard to find in any country. Unfortunately, for personal reasons he had to leave me after too short a stay at the OECD.

Indeed, Jacques Delors, because of his popularity, was long considered the Socialist Party candidate likely to defeat Chirac in the presidential election. However, to the disappointment of millions, as the election approached he declined to run.

Returning to my management meeting, I mentioned President Chirac's preoccupation of the French with the "principe de précaution." Delors laughed and said, "if the precautionary principle is so important to the French, why are we leading the world in generating electricity from nuclear plants?" Interesting point, I thought.

Learning from the failure of the Multilateral Agreement on Investment (MAI), which I discuss below, I convened a special session of all relevant civil society groups. We agreed to share information and expertise throughout a process that would ultimately conclude with a conference in Edinburgh.

The first meeting held at the OECD represented a remarkable cross-section of international interests in agriculture, environmental issues, food distribution, and human health from across the OECD, and many NGOs were present. To ensure that no special interest group or NGO played a dominant role in the discussions, independent journalists were invited to assume the chair.

It was a fascinating discussion, which highlighted the complexity of the GMO issue. Many, like me, had been focusing almost exclusively on possible health concerns. Here is an example. Proponents argued that an advantage of planting GMO crops was that this could intensify agriculture through more production from smaller tracts of land. Mark Avery, speaking on behalf of the UK Royal Society for the Protection of Birds, countered that some bird species were disappearing because agriculture was already more intense than in the past and that GMO crops would only make matters worse. In response, a representative from Latin America argued that they very much needed to intensify production. The alternative, he said, was to expand the amount of arable land by cutting down forests, especially the precious rain forests, one of the planet's most important carbon sinks. This exchange had nothing to do with health or trade but much to do with biodiversity and the environment. Suddenly the complexity of the GMO issue became even greater.

The process of broad-based consultation worked well, even if many issues associated with GMO food production remain.

Moving from trade to investment, the mobility of capital in the latter part of the nineteenth century and the beginning of the twentieth was also enormous. The stock of foreign capital that Western European countries invested in developing countries in 1914 amounted to 32 per cent of GDP compared with 22 per cent in 1998. The period between the two great wars saw the virtual stagnation of foreign direct investment, in part because of the Great Depression.

Like trade, liberalized international investment is a key driver of growth, development, and poverty alleviation. International commitments to investment and responsible corporate behaviour are powerful and critical elements of positive globalization.

Investors taking a long-term perspective expect fair, equitable, and non-discriminatory treatment. Governments, for their part, would like to see the multinational enterprises in their countries behave responsibly as good citizens and in strict accordance with the national regulatory framework.

Despite some negative publicity and a few tragic accidents, most multinational enterprises from the developed world appear to have brought good practices to the countries in which they have established themselves, normally applying the norms and codes of behaviour of their countries of origin. The World Business Council for Sustainable Development, which engages a large percentage of the world's largest multinational companies, sets that as an objective.

To reflect those concerns, the OECD's approach to investment policy traditionally balanced rules aimed at progressive liberalization of investment and standards for corporate behaviour in the Guidelines for Multinational Enterprises.

By 1995, the international framework for investment had become an unwieldy legal jungle of 1,600 bilateral investment agreements

each with its own terms and conditions. It needed pruning to facilitate capital flows, especially to emerging markets and developing
countries, from OECD members, which, at the time, accounted for
nearly all foreign direct investment in the developing world.

THE MULTILATERAL AGREEMENT
ON INVESTMENT CONTROVERSY

To address this complex issue, in 1995 ministers of OECD countries
decided to launch negotiations to establish the controversial MAI. When
I arrived at the OECD in 1996, negotiations were well underway.

At some point a draft was leaked and a number of NGOs decided
to sabotage the entire process, arguing that the negotiating process
had been done in secret and was designed to further the interests
of powerful multinational enterprises at the expense of sovereign
nations. Specious arguments flowed in every direction from many
sources. Misrepresentations repeated and spread by people steeped
in ignorance about the MAI and its objectives began to take hold of
the political process.

Sensing domestic opposition with negative political consequences
generated by NGOs, France backed out of the negotiations in 1998
and others soon followed. There was no point in proceeding.

This was a blow to the eight non-OECD countries that had participated in the negotiations and sought to join the agreement, seeing
it as a way to attract crucial foreign direct investment to their countries. The countries that had participated in the negotiations represented 92 per cent of all outward foreign investment from developed
countries, which is why the OECD was the logical place to hold negotiations. Far from being held in secret, as opposing NGOs argued, the
meetings were a matter of public record, including news releases sent
to journalists.

Although the MAI was quashed, the draft agreement developed
during the OECD negotiations made a significant contribution to
continuing work on investment. It served to identify critical areas
for attracting investment and contributed to the OECD Policy Framework for Investment developed some years later.

The MAI experience also underlined the importance of a good communication strategy including transparency and public consultation. The public by and large does not understand the true nature and the costs and benefits of such policies, which can easily be upended by opponents armed with their own clever communication strategies.

NGOS can combine efforts, usually to good purpose, but sometimes simply to mount political roadblocks to progress. Neither the OECD nor its governments sufficiently communicated the benefits of such an international investment framework. We learned a lesson. It served us well when we later entered the treacherous political area of genetically modified food, which I described above.

THE IMPORTANCE OF GLOBAL
MULTILATERAL FREE TRADE

Returning to trade, will multilateralism, which all countries proclaim to be in the world's best interests, succeed or will it be undermined by bilateral and regional arrangements? The trend to such arrangements (both referred to as regional trade agreements or RTAs) is of great concern if one truly believes in a strong multilateral global trading system.

Consider the following. Successive trade negotiation rounds in the post-war period have brought tariffs lower and lower over a wide range of goods and services. The average tariff in OECD countries on manufactured goods has plummeted since 1950. RTAs like the North American Free Trade Agreement have taken these even lower for the participating countries.

But the RTAs have also created a "spaghetti bowl" of agreements, as prominent economist Jagdish Bhagwati describes them. Any product shipped from one RTA-participating country to another must meet the "rules of origin" requirements to ensure that products from a non-participant are not sneaking through under the advantageous provision of the RTA.

RTAs are major obstacles to the bigger and better world of multilateralism under the WTO, benefiting large economies and locking others out. Consider this: (1) weak economies are not popular candidates for significant RTA participation so they risk being excluded from the wealth-creating benefits of burgeoning global trade; and (2) once in place, an RTA creates vested interests for businesses (and their owners and employees) that do not seek a global market presence and will resist any policy that will invite further competition within the RTA area. This is especially the case with small- and medium-sized enterprises. The same protectionist pressures that benefited the Canadian shoe manufacturer I referred to earlier will be present within the RTA zone, but with a much larger constituency.

During my 2003 visit to Canberra, Australia was negotiating a bilateral free trade agreement with the United States. A journalist asked my opinion of the agreement. As head of the OECD, which by its convention is dedicated to supporting multilateral free trade, I declared that these bilateral agreements were no substitute for a multilateral approach, an opinion the Australian media beamed out to the world.

Robert Zoellick, the US trade representative at the time, who was no doubt engaged in the Australian negotiations, took offence at this position and reproached me at the next annual Ministerial meeting in Paris.

"So," he asked with his customary candour, "you're the multilateral guy who does not like bilateral free trade agreements?"

I reminded him that as a Canadian politician in the 1980s, I had broken ranks with my own political party to vote in favour of a free trade agreement with the United States. I did so because I believed it would be a step in the right direction and that ultimately all RTAs would collapse into a multilateral system under the GATT (the General Agreement on Tariffs and Trade, which was in effect until the WTO was created).

In the absence of a multi-polar world, that prospect is now on the distant horizon. We need more 800-pound gorillas with spheres of influence over trading partners who could put multilateralism back on track. Trade negotiations are a slow and cumbersome process. They are politically and technically complex, even though all countries at the negotiating table should have a coincidence of interests.

Public support for liberalization measures are easier to secure when all countries make substantial contributions to the global effort. The benefits are greater when many countries liberalize trade, although there is evidence that even unilateral action can be beneficial. Measures taken within the framework of transparent and binding rules-based liberalization also provide insurance against protectionist pressures and can add credibility to the efforts of individual countries.

Looking at multilateral trade negotiations, it is important to remember that there is no neat distinction between developed and developing countries. While the OECD is often called the club of rich developed nations, there is immense diversity among its membership. GDP per capita on a purchasing power parity basis in 2013 ranged from a low of $17,302 to a high of $90,809.

Diversity does not end with GDP figures. Policies and trends for trade and investment also differ between OECD countries. Some protect their agricultural sectors, which provide both produce and environmental benefits. Others maintain high industrial tariffs to ward off competition from developing countries that have a comparative advantages through low-cost labour. The OECD countries strong in technologies and services want to penetrate the vast markets of the developing world, while the latter would like tariffs in agricultural and other areas of export potential removed.

Too often in developed countries, narrow sectoral interests block liberalization in certain areas critical to many developing countries. The enormous subsidies paid to American cotton farmers represent a glaring example that takes export opportunities away from developing countries. Sometimes the protection given to one sector can be outrageously expensive and even damaging to another sector in the same country, as illustrated by George Will's comments above.

All countries have an interest in moving toward free trade and investment. Studies by the OECD and others show that countries at all levels of development benefit from free trade and investment.

Trade and foreign direct investment are also powerful mechanisms for the transfer of knowledge and technology between countries. This is becoming even more important in a world of rapid technological innovations and with the emergence of knowledge-based economies.

But liberalization of trade and investment must be on a sustainable basis, consistent with countries' capacity both to adjust and to reap the benefits. To reach those objectives, skilled trade negotiators are necessary. It is a challenge for developing countries to match the depth of skills and experience of negotiators from the large developed economies.

Trade negotiators are unlikely to appreciate the economy wide and international impacts of many comprehensive or even sectorial negotiations. Only senior political leaders can bring that perspective, a point made by Peter Costello, the Australian minister of finance, who told a meeting of OECD trade ministers that sometimes trade issues should be taken out of the hands of technocrats and raised to the political level.

Although leaders attend meetings of APEC, they have seldom attended the important multilateral meetings the WTO. If they had, perhaps the Doha Development Round would have been more successful.

In the late 1990s I explained globalization in various fora as a term bandied about in many ways and in many different contexts. In its simplest form I defined it when fully matured as a borderless economic world. This means that trade and investment on a planetary scale enjoy the same privileges and protections enjoyed within national boundaries. We are a long way from achieving that definition of globalization.

Will we return to the labour-intensive, low-skilled jobs that provided so much low-wage employment in the past, or will we upskill our work forces and ensure that more and more people in the developing world benefit from the increase in the number of jobs in their countries?

I thought we had answered this question when the WTO was created and the Doha Round was launched. In fact, there are many worrying signs that the world is becoming more protectionist, with narrow sector vested interests and concomitant job losses in the Western industrialized countries undermining the society-wide benefits. Some short-sighted politicians could reverse the positive trend toward globalization and the removal of tariffs for the reason described by Bitter Bierce, whom I cited earlier in this chapter: "to protect the domestic producer against the greed of his consumer." That may well include protectionist policies of the kind promoted by President Trump.

14

The Democratic Imperative: Perhaps Not for All?

The comments in this chapter were inspired by a request I received from Korea's *Maeil Business Newspaper*, an outstanding business newspaper with very broad circulation. Specifically, I was asked to answer questions regarding the future of democratic institutions over the next 50 years, with special reference to Korea. The request read as follows: "Our company has always focused on setting an agenda for the Korean society. On this anniversary, we are preparing for a new project for the next 50 years. The theme of the project is 'Future of Politics.' As you are a renowned professional in this field, your candid answers to the following 'two short questions' regarding future politics will be very important for us. It would be of the utmost gratitude if you would respond to them for Korea's political development."

The two questions were effectively combined to ask whether the system based on representative democracy, with the separation of the legislative, executive, and judicial functions, would still be the model in 2050 or whether the model would change, and if so, why.

My initial reaction was one of surprise. I could not imagine such a question being put to me in Canada, the United States, or any of the well-established, mature democracies. But upon reflection I concluded that these questions were not only relevant to Korea but to all countries that are striving to maintain robust democratic government or that are hoping to become sustainable democracies. They invoked in my mind Winston Churchill's famous statement: "Democracy is the worst form of government, except for all the others."

The questions made me realize that I had thus far neglected a fundamental question that the journalists at the *Maeil Business Newspaper* had posed. I wondered why. Had I not been exposed to varying forms of democracy across the planet? What lessons could be drawn from that experience? Had I not seen traditional representation by duly-elected representatives influenced and sometimes overturned by non-elected forces that had often coalesced through the use of the power of the Internet and social networking, which were tools not even dreamt of when I was first elected to the federal Canadian Parliament in 1978?

My experience in Thailand in 2005 when I was invited to meet with the Thai prime minister, Thaksin Shinawatra, comes to mind. I was astonished to find Shinawatra's office building surrounded by protesters seeking his resignation. I was escorted by security personnel to his office. The prime minister greeted me warmly, seemingly unconcerned by the noisy protesters. We engaged in casual conversation over coffee, and after an exchange of views on the Thai economy, I inquired about the motives of the protesters. He smiled and said, "They are organized by my opponent, who used to be an ally. Tomorrow, my supporters from the regions outside of Bangkok will replace them."

Having been duly elected by the people of Thailand, he was the first democratically elected prime minister to serve a full term and was re-elected in 2005 by an overwhelming majority. But he was overthrown by a military coup in 2006.

Democracy only works as it should when all accept the results of an honest election. That did not happen in Thailand, a fledgling democracy. This is why independent observers are important to ensure that results are not rigged, normally by the party in power, which is in a position to do so.

I concluded that the questions from the Korean newspaper are important, not just for Korea but for all democracies. For this reason, I thought it would be useful to include in this book the answers I sent to the Korean journalists, along with some personal reflections on additional phenomena that are changing the notion of representational government as my generation and the generations of my parents and grandparents have known it.

First, here is how I responded to the Korean journalists:

As the great economist Keynes reminded us, examine the present in light of the past for the purposes of the future. I have found that advice to be very useful, especially in assessing how political systems are likely to evolve. This is especially true in mature democracies that have developed constitutions and practices for generations, which are more easily seen as building on the past with a wealth of precedents and experience to draw upon. They are designed to defeat forces wishing to undermine the constitution, whether from civil society or the military.

This does not mean that there cannot be abrupt and unforeseen changes that can have a profound effect on the political systems, although they are less likely to undermine the fundamental democratic principles rooted in the history and democratic culture of the citizenry.

For example, one of the oldest and most robust democracies is that of the United States. Currently it is going through a serious crisis of what many call " money politics" where the capacity to influence the election of candidates through massive financial contributions to publicity campaigns has made many Americans feel that government has become "for the rich, by the rich." If corrective measures are not introduced soon, the United States may face a revolution because those who have been disenfranchised through money politics will regard the political process itself as corrupt. However, I am reasonably confident that this absurd situation will not endure because it is so contrary to the political culture of mainstream American thinking.

Applying Keynes' formula to South Korea is much more difficult because it is a very young democracy. Think of this. Park Geun-hye, president from 2013 to 2017, witnessed her own father assassinated as president in 1979 and a coup d'état followed under General Chun Doo-hwan, who became president. It was not until 1987 that Roh Tae-woo said he would support democratization and direct election of the president.

Since then we have seen a number of successive presidential

democratic elections. I have had the privilege of meeting five presidents and often working closely with some, especially Kim Dae-jung.

Has the culture of democracy now established firm roots in South Korea? We should hope so, but it requires much vigilance to ensure that it has, and that a strong, fair, and transparent democracy remains the way forward.

Other countries have moved to become democracies and then begun to backslide in a worrisome manner. Take Thailand as an example. In 1992 the military government was brought down. The country was doing well economically, with a strong, well-educated middle class, and after several elections in the late 1990s it had adopted a reformist constitution. Today it appears to be a failed democracy because the kind of vigilance by civil society that was activated in the early 1990s seems to have disappeared, with the military once again playing a predominant role.

Turkey is another example. A secular democratic state was established by Mustafa Kemal Atatürk in the 1930s, which was safeguarded by the military until recent years.

President Erdoğan seems determined to reverse much of the secularism that Atatürk accomplished and seems to have moved against the media with more and more journalists in jail. According to a report published by the Committee to Protect Journalists, Turkish authorities are engaging in widespread criminal prosecution and jailing of journalists and are applying other forms of severe pressure to promote self-censorship in the press.

I cite these examples just to illustrate how the unthinkable can happen to undermine democracies, often stimulated by a strong leader who is able to control the military or the media and undermine the judiciary with the tacit agreement of a compliant society.

There is a thoughtful but disquieting essay in an edition of *Foreign Affairs* entitled "Why Personalism Rules" (26 September 2016). The authors suggest that personalized systems of governments are growing across the globe: "Data show that personalism is on the rise worldwide. And although the trend has been widespread, it has been most pronounced in authoritarian settings. Data show that personalist dictatorships – or those regimes where power is highly concentrated in the hands of a single individual – have increased notably since the end of the Cold War. In 1988, personalist regimes comprised 23 percent of all dictatorships. Today, 40 percent of all autocracies are ruled by strongmen."

This worrisome trend suggests that the tripartite approach attributed to Montesquieu in his seminal work *Spirit of Laws* (1748), which involves checks and balances through the separation of the executive, legislative, and judiciary functions of government, is not well established in many of these countries. Strongmen seem able to usurp the powers of other branches though different mechanisms.

South Korea, and indeed all democracies, must ensure that those checks and balances are robust and supported by a competent and dedicated public service. The government must have as an anchor a respected, competent, and independent judiciary that will protect and defend the constitution whether it is attacked from another branch of government, such as the military, or by third-party interests.

Certain aspects of democracies are difficult to control. For example, how does one ensure that the citizenry will largely exercise the precious right to vote? In a number of countries voting is mandatory, such as Argentina, Australia, Belgium, Bolivia, and Brazil.

This practice might sometimes be worth considering in countries where there seems to be voter apathy. Perhaps this option should also be examined in countries that do not have a long history of democracy, such as South Korea. It might focus the general public more closely on the important public policy issues.

I believe that in all countries the legislators should have close oversight of the military, police forces, and departments of justice to ensure that basic civil liberties and especially the freedom of the media are safeguarded. The situation in Russia and Turkey, where the media seems to be under attack if not supportive of government positions, is very dangerous. Sometimes, when countries find themselves with weak opposition in legislatures it is the members of the fourth estate (the media) who must provide constructive and critical opposition. Their independence allows them to provide a further check to add to Montesquieu's tripartite system.

Finally, a word about the importance of the public service in ensuring the continuity and integrity of good government and in supporting the objective implementation of the policies of elected officials. To avoid corrupt practices and function effectively, governments must develop high-quality, well-trained, and well-paid incorruptible public servants.

My encounters with public servants across the globe during my career have convinced me that a highly trained, well-remunerated, dedicated, and honest public service is the only way to ensure honest, effective, and competent public and private sectors. No government can effectively forward its social and economic agendas without a first-class public service.

A major concern of all democracies must be the adoption of policies addressing the long-term health of society as a whole and, in the case of climate change, the biosphere as a whole. The entire planet is at serious risk in the years ahead, but the democratic electoral processes have not served us well because politicians are not inclined to take into account the welfare of future generations in the next election. This is a major challenge for all of us. The future should have a constituency today.

The short-termism in politics may be tempered to some degree by the public service, which should have a longer term view. I see no force other than fear of apocalyptic weather events that can change political thinking, as the public at large becomes more conscious of what is at stake. A good, credible public service may be able to move the challenge of addressing issues like climate change off the political agenda into a nonpartisan framework. Could Korea show the world how this might be accomplished? It has taken many green initiatives and currently hosts the Global Green Growth Institute.

In conclusion, never take good democratic government for granted and ensure that the Korean students of today become leaders of tomorrow with an understanding of the fragility of the tripartite balance, which they must maintain with the assistance of a strong fourth, and perhaps fifth, estate. The fourth estate is now supplemented by the so-called fifth estate of blogging, social networking, and other creations of the information and communication societies in which we all live.

It would be presumptuous of me to suggest an inventory of specific governmental initiatives for Korea as it moves forward to 2050 and beyond. What I have touched upon are some principles rather than prescriptions.

However, I do believe that democracy is best defended and strengthened by those who believe strongly in its capacity to bring prosperity and more equality to society as a whole. My concern is that, too often, those concerns are not expressed at the ballot box.

Korean children must learn, and all our children must learn, that healthy democracy does not happen by accident. They must understand from an early age that their future depends upon their willingness to engage and make sacrifices in time and money to ensure that through a broadly engaged political process, Korea takes its place among the truly democratic countries and does not "slide backwards" as some countries seem to be doing.

Koreans continue to prove that they place a very high value on innovation and adaptation. They have done this through good education, hard work, and sacrifice. Since the financial crisis of 1997–98 Korea has more than doubled its GDP, something thought by OECD economists to be without precedent.

I am optimistic that Koreans have learned from the lessons of their history and will bring their skills of innovation and adaptation to good governance at all levels within a strong democracy tailored to their own specific social, cultural, and economic imperatives. This is important, not only for Koreans, but for the world.

In responding to those questions I realized how fragile democracy can be and how easily it can be undermined and even destroyed by people who, once legitimately elected, can manipulate critical components of the government apparatus, such as a truly independent judiciary, to their benefit unless there is effective opposition and a robust independent democratic election process. Never forget that Adolf Hitler was initially elected.

SOCIAL MEDIA TRUMPS POLITICIANS

I believe that governments in this century have an enormous challenge to make democracy work for all, not just the often-derided 1 per cent who hold as much as 80 per cent of national wealth around the globe (in some countries this group holds more of the wealth, in others less). Adding to the challenge faced by representative governments is the necessity to deal with NGOs, which often represent very specific single interests. NGOs have changed the political landscape. That is not in itself a bad thing for the democratic process, but the influence of NGOs must be managed to improve, not obstruct, democracy.

My generation largely believed that we should entrust decisions on major economic and societal issues to those representatives elected by the people. They had access to information and expertise not available on a daily basis to the general public. These resources are more available to the public today, but more often than not in a controversial context. So there is a new and perhaps dangerous threat to representative government as propounded by Edmund Burke in the nineteenth century, namely the voice of "civil society" offered by many NGOs and amplified considerably by the media and the Internet.

Communication technology is having a profound impact on the classic democratic model. NGOs also have an important role to play in the new communication world, provided they are willing to act responsibly. The problem is that leaders of NGOs, unlike elected politicians, do not represent a societal consensus view on the subject they choose to promote or oppose: often they are single-issue proponents.

For example, on energy, an NGO may be against nuclear energy, against fossil fuels, and against carbon capture and sequestration and may strongly support alternative energies (e.g., wind, solar, hydro) but may not take into account the fact that none of these alternative energies is capable of meeting the world's base load energy require-ments. NGOs may ignore the numbers and usually do not offer alter-natives, as politicians must. Some refuse to recognize current reali-ties, simply saying that we must change our lifestyles. This is a great idea, but it is neither an acceptable nor a practical political response.

Yes, Churchill's comment about democracy being "the worst form of government, except for all the others" has been proven to be right by the obvious success of robust democracies, which have consistently outperformed all other systems both economically and in terms of societal progress.

I repeat: democracy is very fragile and it requires constant vigi-lance to keep it healthy and responsive to changing economic and societal demands. That is true for all democracies, but it is a greater challenge where the system has no historic roots and where the coun-try has a culture of changing leadership and direction not through elections but rather through a disruptive overthrow by revolution, either quiet like the one in Thailand or brutal like the one in France in 1789.

There is a disquieting commentary in the *New York Times* of 16 December 2016 entitled "Is Donald Trump a Threat to Democracy" by Professors Steven Levitsky and Daniel Ziblatt of Harvard Univer-sity. Here is an excerpt:

> Donald J. Trump's election has raised a question that few Americans ever imagined asking: Is our democracy in danger? … Past stability is no guarantee of democracy's future survival … Our research points to several warning signs.
>
> The clearest warning sign is the ascent of anti-democratic politicians into mainstream politics. Drawing on a close study of democracy's demise in 1930s Europe, the eminent political scientist Juan J. Linz designed a "litmus test" to identify anti-democratic politicians. His indicators include a failure to reject violence unambiguously, a readiness to curtail rivals' civil liber-ties, and the denial of the legitimacy of elected governments.
>
> Mr. Trump tests positive. In the campaign, he encouraged violence among supporters; pledged to prosecute Hillary Clinton;

threatened legal action against unfriendly media; and suggested that he might not accept the election results.

Yes, democracy can be fragile everywhere.

The questions from Korea woke me up to the reality that no democracy can be taken for granted. We who live in well-established democracies must never be complacent or smug about the success of our societies. The comments of the Harvard professors above implicitly echo that concern.

Our democratic societies and their political systems must adapt to a rapidly evolving world. We are increasingly in McLuhan's global village.

In line with the work of Charles Darwin, it has been said that "it is not the strongest of the species that survive, nor the most intelligent, but the one most responsive to change." The same could be said of democratic governments and even empires.

15

Can the Tide Return?

That men do not learn very much from the lessons of history is the most important of all the lessons of history.

Aldous Huxley

In the preface I outlined the extraordinary challenges and opportunities the world's leaders faced toward the end of the twentieth century. At the risk of some repetition it is helpful to remind ourselves of where we were 20 years ago with respect to some of the key questions that were on the global agenda at the time and where we are today.

Twenty years ago, we looked forward to:

1   establishing vibrant democracies in former communist states;
2   supporting global free trade with effective and transparent corporate governance;
3   eliminating poverty in the world;
4   eradicating pervasive corruption;
5   supporting the further evolution of a coherent and powerful EU;
6   extending the formula of the Marshall Plan to other regions of the world; and
7   coming to grips with the challenges of climate change.

These goals were seen at the time to be not only desirable but also attainable. They were not perceived as in the poetry of Robert Browning: "Ah, but a man's reach should exceed his grasp." Each of the priorities on that agenda was within our grasp.

I wrote this book to illustrate where and why we failed to realize nearly all of those objectives, with the possible exception of using a Marshall Plan approach to secure peace in the Balkans, which seems to be holding. We need to remind ourselves of the following things:

1   We failed to engage Russia with the West and as a result are now strengthening NATO in an effort to contain Putin's aggressive behaviour. History may show this to be the most egregious of all Western public policy failures in the post-Soviet Union period, as outlined in chapter 4, because of its impact on other areas of global concern where Russia should have been a partner.

2   The EU is increasingly fragile, with concern about the future of the euro common currency and the EU's capacity to deal with massive immigration from the war-torn areas of the Middle East.

3   Tensions have grown between China and its neighbours over territorial disputes, convincing the United States to pivot from its European focus and increase its military presence in Asia.

4   There is a risk of reigniting the Cold War my generation grew up with.

5   The global free trade agenda is in the doldrums with the failure of the Doha Round and the concomitant rise of protectionist rhetoric, especially in the United States at the highest political levels.

6   The prospect of eliminating poverty in the developing world through trade and investment is dying.

7   Reductions in GHG emissions, especially CO_2, continue to elude us after decades of effort, showing how ineffectual the United Nations Framework Convention on Climate Change process has been and will be. The widely heralded but unenforceable Paris Agreement in the context of a history of failures is even dangerous because much of the public thinks our leaders have come to grips with this challenge (as we all did after the Kyoto Protocol was adopted in 1997). They do not realize that even if the agreed-upon targets are achieved they are not sufficient to keep global mean

temperatures below the level that the scientific community tells us is necessary to prevent dramatic and irreversible climate change. There is resistance to developing a Plan B as a last resort to prevent unacceptable global warming. In addition, there is growing concern about the increase in emissions of methane, which contributes much more to global warming than CO_2 but fortunately has a shorter atmospheric life. The position that the Trump administration takes about curbing GHG emissions will be pivotal in preventing serious and damaging long-term global warming. Initial statements are not encouraging.

8   For those who believe in democracy and perceived it beginning to take root after the fall of the Berlin Wall and the collapse of the Soviet Union, there is surely profound disappointment. In some countries, such as Thailand, there has been a return to a military dictatorship. In others, such as Russia and other countries that were formerly part of the Soviet Union, there is only a pretense of democracy. There also appears to be backsliding in Turkey, a very important global player and a bridge between Asia and its historic Western allies.

THE TIDE OF OPPORTUNITIES HAS EBBED

In summary, what looked to be a promising future in all the major areas of concern in the 1990s has evolved into what could best be described as an economic, social, and geopolitical mess. But as bad as that story is, we have succeeded in making the future even more problematic with the arrival of global terrorism. While this global destabilizing threat appears to be a direct product of the Bush administration's aggression in Iraq and the unleashing of the latent hostilities within the Islamic world, there are some who will see this as a validation of the late Samuel Huntington's thesis "The clash of civilizations."

After his death in late 2008, the *Harvard Gazette* (5 February 2009) summarized Huntington's controversial view, which he first put forward in 1992: "He argued that in a post-Cold War world, violent conflict would come not from ideological friction between nation states, but from cultural and religious differences among the world's major civilizations." We should hope that Huntington was wrong, but the collapse of the Arab Spring and the continuing conflicts in the Middle East combined with the spread of terrorism may encourage many in the Western nations who harbour anti-Islamic sentiments to view Huntington as prophetic.

The reality is that we confront terrorist suicide bombers who undoubtedly dream of acquiring nuclear weapons and using them against Western nations. Much better was the Cold War world of MAD (mutually assured destruction), which at least created a balance of power through fear of retaliation.

TIDES CAN RETURN

Throughout this volume I have attempted to identify some lessons learned. The principal ones can be summarized as follows.

Economic interdependence and cooperation and the benefits derived from them bring lasting peace and prosperity, as they have in continental Europe. The lessons of the Marshall Plan are as relevant today as they were following the Second World War. They should be used to bring the Middle East and North Africa region together when armed conflict is resolved and also to engage Israel as a partner. Similarly, economic interdependence should resolve the tensions in Asia, including North Korea.

"Know what you do not know" and admit to it. Economists and others who influence public policy must set aside bias against counterintuitive ideas and base their recommendations on facts, not assumptions; decision making on the basis of assumptions brought on the disastrous Iraq war and its continuing consequences. That hubris, shared by many economists, also seems to have contributed mightily to the global economic meltdown of 2007–08. I quoted Anatole Kaletsky in chapter 6, and it is worth doing so again here: "The economics profession must bear a lot of the blame for the current crisis. If it is to become useful again it must undergo an intellectual revolution – becoming both broader and more modest."

Politicians must take politically difficult decisions that often require major structural reforms early in their mandates so that the electorate will see the benefits before the next election. Turkey's Erdoğan did and maintained his popularity. Germany's Schroeder waited too long. To support such decisions, politicians must develop understandable communication strategies illustrating the benefits that best serve the long-term public interest. Too often in democracies, short-term political imperatives trump long-term economic and societal considerations. Both the benefits of trade and investment as well as the challenge of climate change have been poorly communicated to the public and advances on both of these fronts continue to be undermined by vacuous demagoguery.

Leaders should not overreach, as 190 countries have done in fruitless efforts to finalize an international free trade agreement known as the Doha Round or as almost 200 countries have done in their efforts to find consensus on concrete solutions to address the challenges of climate change. Neither set of efforts, the first initiated through the WTO process and the second through the United Nations Framework Convention on Climate Change process, has delivered the results sought and it is unlikely they ever will. Starting small and gradually broadening an international consensus is probably a better option. The EU successfully evolved from a small base but it appears to have expanded too rapidly to consolidate and build upon its remarkable and successful beginnings. Even the G20 may be ineffectual because of size and economic and social diversity.

The difficulty of building broad consensus on these issues suggests that a structure more resembling the UN Security Council would be more effective. For example, there could be four permanent members: the United States, the Russian Federation, the EU, and China. There could be added four non-permanent members on a limited-term basis. Even without non-permanent members, if the four permanent members could reach consensus they could constitute a steering group for the global community. Whether we like it or not, each of these four powers has major spheres of influence over smaller regional powers through shared history, culture (sometimes language), and trade and investment.

Some reject the notion of spheres of influence as a throwback to the United States' Monroe Doctrine of 1823, which was invoked by President Kennedy as recently as the Cuban Missile Crisis in 1962. Current US foreign policy declares the era of the Monroe Doctrine to be over. But the reality is that each of the four powers has important spheres of influence and could help bring countries within those spheres into a consensus for policy action on such issues as trade and climate change.

We have also witnessed the regional and even global impact of domestic micro market failures. When there is a failure to identify and deal with them expeditiously they can balloon into a macro crisis with international implications because of the international integration of financial markets. We witnessed this regionally with the 1997 Asian crisis but globally with the subprime derivative crisis. This risk calls for stronger and better surveillance at the structural level as well as more emphasis on financial education for the general population.

Globalization has created incredible interdependence of markets, not just financial markets, so that policies that depress markets of major trading partners have a broad knock-on effect, the breadth depending on the size and importance of the market affected. That is why the debate in the United States on how to deal with the most serious recession since the 1930s was so important for the global economy. I discussed this at length in chapter 8. The lesson learned is critical.

It is important to keep public finances in balance, but if unforeseen events tip the scales and public spending risks increasing deficits, leaders should be wary of "hair shirt" austerity prescriptions. Consider the negative effects of these nostrums on entrepreneurial activity and small businesses with liquidity needs, on outward migration, and on the morale of the general population. Selective public investment during a serious economic downturn can and has provided short-term employment, long-term productivity, and greater future government revenues. Witness the performance of the United States following the 2008 recession with the Troubled Asset Relief Program and the extensive use of quantitative easing by the US Federal Reserve Board to provide necessary liquidity to ensure renewed economic growth and job creation.

Leaders must attack the corruption that undermines economic growth and condemns millions in the developing world to live in poverty. Even in developed economies, corruption reduces public confidence in, and respect for, democratic institutions and the political process. It is tragic that in wonderful countries like Russia and other former members of the Soviet Union, corruption continues to hold back the economic growth and prosperity of their peoples.

A government can only be as good as the quality and professional competence of its public service. Investment in such human capital is crucial to ensuring honest and effective government in both the public and private sectors.

Healthy democracies have proven their value in supporting economic and social progress across the planet. Unfortunately, many of our fellow travellers have yet to enjoy the individual freedom and satisfaction that democracy can bring. It is a fragile flower of recent creation. In newly emerging democracies it sometimes has shallow roots that politicians and influential citizens should support and protect. This has not happened in Russia and in other former members of the Soviet Union where it was thought that democracy would succeed after the fall of the Berlin Wall. We see backsliding even in Poland and Hungary. The situation in Turkey, which held such promise only a decade ago, is also worrisome. President Erdoğan seems increasingly autocratic and intolerant of criticism and dissent. Failure of this democracy could be a sad, even tragic, development. Turkey is a major regional and global power, and through the influence of Atatürk it became an emerging secular democracy with a majority Sunni population straddling Europe and Asia. Atatürk showed the world what individual leadership supported by ethical standards could accomplish.

I was asked by the Turkish government to write a tribute to him in 1999. It read, in part: "Mustafa Kemal (Atatürk) is one of the most remarkable leaders of the 20th century. A liberal thinker well ahead of his time, he transformed a large and complex country in a way and at a pace that is probably unique in history. He combined passion, compassion, courage, liberalism, and style in a manner we have not seen since his premature death in 1938 ... Young Turks today should look no further than Mustafa Kemal, remembered as Atatürk, to set their compasses for the future. So should the rest of us."

With optimism about the future of "global" democratic governments in retreat, the youth of all countries must learn the importance of democratic freedoms at an early age and be urged to participate actively in the democratic process.

Leaders must recognize and seize opportunities to change the course of history for the better. The evolution of Russia after the collapse of the Soviet Union is a remarkable example of a failure to do so. Perhaps not bringing Turkey into the family of European nations within the EU may have contributed to the current instability and concern for Turkey's future. There is fear that President Erdoğan is attempting to reverse the incredible achievements of Atatürk and remake Turkey as a non-democratic Islamic majority Sunni state. It is too early to tell whether those widely shared fears are justified.

In addition to these substantive lessons, we should appreciate the importance of communicating public policy options effectively through the media to the people. We have seen excellent policies fail when they are "lost in translation."

Despite the dismal period in which we find ourselves today, one in which no society is safe from international terrorism and where protectionism and geopolitical tensions seem on the rise, will we use these lessons to build a better future?

We missed the tide of opportunity in the 1990s. Will there be another tide that could bring us to where we should be as opposed to where we are? If the tide does return, the opportunities it brings must be seized and guided by the will of dedicated, honest, and intelligent leaders and not left by the wayside.

Appendix:
The Benefits of International Conferences

We live in a world of meetings. There are commercial, professional, and cultural conventions, industrial showcases, scientific and social workshops, and political gatherings: an alphabet soup of gatherings covering every conceivable area of human endeavour. Rarely do I enter a major hotel that has any kind of meeting facility, however modest, without seeing a posted list of events bringing together people from across the country or, often, from around the world. At every major airport a line of chauffeurs and greeters hold up signs with names of companies, events, or individual VIPs who are to be escorted to their conference hotel or other destination.

This is not a new phenomenon, but I believe that globalization combined with the ease of national and international travel has dramatically increased these diverse gatherings. Skeptics and cynics characterize many of these events as chat shops, with few attendees taking the panel discussions or keynote addresses by prominent personages seriously. Many escape to network in the corridors, bars, and coffee shops.

I do not denigrate the tsunami of international events that bring together senior politicians, corporate leaders, prominent journalists, Nobel Prize winners, and heads of international organizations. On the contrary, I have come to see this event engagement as a positive force contributing much to international integration, mutual understanding, and the long term health of the global community. Obviously events are not all of equal value, but I believe they have helped to establish lasting networks and friendships between individuals, organizations, and, through the political class, societies.

I recall, during my time as a cabinet minister in the Trudeau government, a discussion with the remarkable Frank Scott, a professor, poet, and ardent social reformer central to the creation of the Canadian socialist political movement. Despite our differing political and economic views we had become close friends. Our conversation took place when the fabric of Canada was being seriously threatened by the Quebec separatist movement. Knowing Frank's perception of a badly regulated market economy and his misgivings about the motives of the Canadian business community, I was surprised by his comment: "Don, despite my serious reservations about the motives of most business leaders, I have to admit that national corporations have done more to weave together the people of this country than have governments at all levels."

He recognized that the transfer and intermingling of personnel within major Canadian corporations had woven a fabric of understanding and friendship that was unlikely to be destroyed by political forces in the long run. Events were part of that national bonding, and he could have added professional associations of lawyers, doctors, accountants, and many others.

As secretary-general of the OECD, I joined the international community of event attendees. The same phenomenon that Frank had observed at the national level in Canada was also happening internationally, thanks to globalization, and it was having the same positive consequences.

Political posturing and megaphone diplomacy between political leaders generate provocative media headlines but rarely reflect the reality of strong relationships among the international groups of like-minded people. These global communities of interest, with common concerns and goals, rise above petty political posturing.

What better example than the anti-French sentiments nurtured by the Bush administration during the US invasion of Iraq. Calling for freedom fries and bans on French products, some Americans bought the anti-French rhetoric but I never sensed that it had negatively affected the strong relationships between the French and American peoples in all walks of life. And our communities of interest? They continued to meet at international events, returning home with a large array of business cards and a head full of innovative ideas.

A number of events with a global reach are regular features on the international calendar. I have been privileged to attend many during my time in public life, as a minister, then as secretary-general, and later as a panellist and speaker. Examples include the World Economic Forum in Davos created by the remarkable Klaus Schwab. The premier event of its kind, it has grown from modest beginnings as the European Management Forum to a "must" on the calendar of many politicians, bankers, economists, academics, media stars, and NGOs from all over the world.

My first experience with Klaus Schwab and his Forum, as it was then known, dates back to 1982 when I was a Canadian minister. At the time it was a small gathering. Political personalities like Ted Heath, Raymond Barre, and Hans-Dietrich Genscher played active roles but, as I recall, my only fellow Canadian was a representative of the Royal Bank of Canada based in London. Klaus Schwab is the international impresario of all time; he filled Davos with heads of state as well as the movers and shakers in the worlds of business, economy, academia, science, and entertainment. I attended the Davos Forum for a total of 12 years, enjoying the opportunity to exchange views on everything from education to biotechnology with Bill Gates, Michael Dell, Newt Gingrich, John Kerry, Kofi Annan, Yasser Arafat, and leading industrialists, bankers, Nobel laureates, and economists.

Rather less enjoyable were my meetings with the Swiss president or the minister of finance who took advantage of my presence in Davos to berate me in a polite but quite aggressive way about the OECD's work on harmful tax practices and tax evasion. They saw it as an assault on the integrity of their banking system, which protected the identity of clients, and their legal system, which did not criminalize tax evasion.

Though we did not use the term *globalization* in 1982, I believe that Schwab and the World Economic Forum have greatly contributed to it. The non-threatening, non-partisan environment of Davos promotes personal connections that carry short-term and long-term benefits to people around the world.

The World Knowledge Forum in Korea, created by Dae-Whan Chang, publisher of the *Maeil Business Newspaper* and owner of two TV channels, has grown significantly since its inception in 2000. For those interested in Asia, particularly Northeast Asia, this is a not-to-miss event. As in Davos, the World Knowledge Forum offers an opportunity to engage with interesting personalities. For example, a few years ago I had dinner and breakfast with Sarah Palin and then with the dynamic former mayor of Los Angeles, Antonio Villaraigosa.

The China Development Forum is of significant interest given China's growing influence in the world. The Chinese Development Research Centre, under the capable organization of Lu Mai, established the Forum in 2000, and it is open only to invitees. I attended six of these annual events, listening to speeches and participating in candid discussions about China and its development. In a smaller session, there was a question and answer with the incumbent prime minister. In my case, that was Zhu Rongji followed by Wen Jiabao. The day often ended in the Great Hall with entertainment provided by talented Chinese singers and dancers.

The International Economic Forum of the Americas began humbly as the Montreal Economic Forum. Founded in 1995 by Gil Rémillard, a constitutional lawyer and former Quebec cabinet member, this is a North American style Davos, which he has succeeded in making an important and stimulating annual event.

I created the annual OECD Forum in 2000 to coincide with the annual Ministerial meeting of member countries. Held in the OECD's Paris headquarters, it has been a resounding success that enables policy messages from civil society to be delivered in real time to senior decision makers from capitals. In 2014 the Forum attracted 1,900 participants from nearly 70 countries, 190 high-level speakers, and more than 200 journalists.

Why did I create this forum? The lack of a good communication strategy for the Multilateral Agreement on Investment, which was intended to complement the trade agenda by establishing a framework for international business investment, made it apparent that the OECD should have engaged civil society in discussions about this important public policy instrument at the outset.

Drafting of the agreement was well underway before my term as secretary-general and I saw it as a logical and useful addition to the globalization agenda of the OECD members. Unfortunately, a number of NGOs who had the power to frighten politicians disagreed. Our talented head of publications and communications, Chris Brooks, suggested that a Forum coinciding with the annual Ministerial meeting would provide an excellent opportunity for NGOs to confer with decision makers. I agreed, and the rest is history.

The Munich Security Conference deserves special mention because it illustrates how valuable such meetings can be. This annual conference on international security policy has been taking place since 1963 and is now the world's largest gathering of its kind. An independent forum for the exchange of views by international security policy decision makers, it brings together some 350 senior figures from more than 70 countries around the world to engage in an intensive debate on current and future security challenges. Managed since 2009 by the capable and distinguished former German ambassador Wolfgang Ischinger, it undoubtedly contributed to keeping the Cold War cold by bringing adversaries together in an atmosphere conducive to building trust through frank exchanges on critical security issues. In the current international environment it may once again be a significant contributor to constructive dialogue between presumed adversaries.

Other events of note are the Astana Economic Forum, the St Petersburg International Economic Forum, and the World Policy Conference created by Thierry de Montbrial (founder of the pre-eminent French think-tank the French Institute of International Relations), which, unlike the others, is held in different locations each year.

I have had the privilege and pleasure of attending all of these events and highly recommend them to people interested in public policy and in strengthening international relations.

Index